AF395489

Heimrad Bäcker

Documentary Poetry

EDITED AND TRANSLATED BY PATRICK GREANEY

Winter Editions, 2024

ON HEIMRAD BÄCKER'S DOCUMENTARY POETICS

Between 1985 and 1997, Heimrad Bäcker (1925–2003) published four books of concrete and documentary poetry almost entirely composed with quotations from texts related to the Shoah: *SEASCAPE* (1985), *transcript* (1986), *epitaph* (1989), and *transcript 2* (1997). He drew on his collection of source material that he began assembling in the late 1940s from Nazi publications, internal Nazi memoranda, the Nuremberg trial proceedings, postwar historical studies, and accounts by victims and perpetrators. Beginning in 1968, Bäcker also pursued his documentation of the Shoah through photographs he took on the grounds of the concentration camp Mauthausen and its subcamps Gusen and St. Georgen, which were only a twenty-minute drive from his home in Linz. The writings collected here are his published attempts to theorize the poetics that shaped his writing and his photography.

Bäcker describes his writing as an act of "reflection" that transposes words and word patterns from the Nazi killing system into what he called his "transcript system." This transposition shows how everyday utterances are tied to the Shoah—speech that ranges from casual remarks to technical and euphemistic formulations designed to facilitate and conceal mass murder. Bäcker focused on statements like "i need more freight trains if i'm going to take care of things quickly," quoted from a 1943 letter from Heinrich Himmler, and "you will find my body before you get to the school, it's by the street watchman's house," taken from a collection of last letters from executed resistance fighters.

In the sources for these quotations, these sentences might not stand out. But encountered on an otherwise blank page, Himmler's desire "to take care of things" and the victim's phrase "my body" can be thought and felt in relation to what Bäcker calls the "tremendum" of the Shoah. This relation is for Bäcker the true sense of "concrete," understood in its philosophical sense as the unification of the particular and the universal. For Bäcker, writing was an act of concretion that revealed a murderous system at work in linguistic details.

There is no need, Bäcker writes, to add accusations or judgments to his quotations. A condemnation from the outside would imply that its underlying moral principles survived the Shoah intact, which Bäcker doubted. The everyday language of bureaucrats, ordinary Germans, and even the worst Nazi criminals was full of moralizing intentions and concepts. Most of them thought and spoke of themselves as idealists acting for the good of humanity. In "Documentary Poetry," Bäcker refers to a speech given by Himmler, who, as head of the SS, was among the most responsible for planning and carrying out the Shoah. In 1943, he spoke about the "extermination of the Jewish people" to an audience of ninety-two SS officers in the German-occupied Polish town of Posen: "Most of you know what it means to have 100 corpses lying next to each other, or 500 or 1000. To have held up through this, and to remain decent ... this has toughened us. This is a glorious chapter in our history, one that has never been written and never will be written." For Himmler, decency and glory went together perfectly with mass graves. "The road to Auschwitz was paved with righteousness," as historian Claudia Koonz puts it in her book *The Nazi Conscience*. National Socialism's idealistic façade, Bäcker insists, tainted the ideals that might have been used against it.

Bäcker's reflections point to the quoted utterances' historicity: their place in human history and the fact that, as an actualization of humanity's enduring potential, they could be spoken again as part of a murderous practice today or tomorrow. Bäcker is most eloquent about this in his text about Mauthausen. He describes his photographs of the camp as an effort to restore historicity to the landscape and industrial areas whose relation to the Shoah was disappearing, as Austrian authorities had refused to include in the Mauthausen Memorial the vast industrial complex and swaths of land that were once part of the main camp and its subcamps.

The history at the center of Bäcker's poetry and photography was part of his own past. He was an enthusiastic Nazi during the years when Austria was part of Nazi Germany (1938 to 1945), working in the Hitler Youth leadership and publishing in a local newspaper. This was also when he began to take photographs. In his publications as an adult, Bäcker highlights this part of his biography. He cites his own adolescent texts in *transcript* and in the afterword to *epitaph*, and the back flap of *transcript 2* lists the details of his participation in Nazism: "Heimrad Bäcker, born in 1925 in Vienna, lives in Linz. 1941–1943, trainee in the local section of the *Linzer Tages-Post* newspaper, then staff member of the Hitler Youth Leadership for the Upper Danube Region. Last rank: Second Lieutenant. Joined the Party at 18." He also included photos from his Hitler Youth days in his retrospective

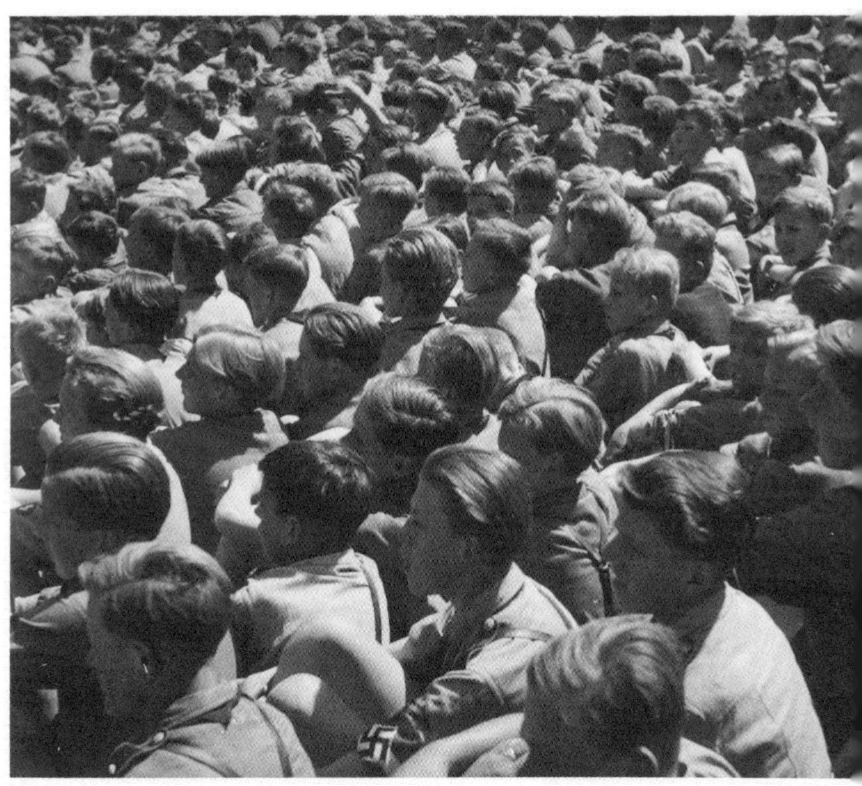

Closing Ceremonies, 1943/1944

exhibition held in Linz in 2002. As Stephan Steiner and Judith Veichtlbauer say in the interview translated here, it is difficult to think of another German or Austrian author who writes anything like this about their participation in the Nazi regime, let alone an author who declares their Party membership on a book jacket.

Bäcker dedicated the rest of his life to the critique of the movement that he supported in his youth. Although his works about Nazism were only published in the 1980s, his 1973 text on concrete poetry shows that he was already

thinking about avant-garde writing as a critique of Nazism.
He discusses concrete poetry as a reaction against "preformed speech," which he ties to "the virtue and hygiene
of the white race." His historical references in that text
differ markedly from other concrete poets of his generation. Instead of Mallarmé and Apollinaire, he names as his
precursors literary works that use montage and citation
to refer to political and historical events, like Büchner's
Danton's Death, Döblin's *Berlin Alexanderplatz*, Helmut
Heissenbüttel's "Germany 1944," and Friedrich Achleitner's "preparations for an execution."

Bäcker published most of his concrete and documentary poetry in his sixties and seventies, after a long period
of study in which he eked out an existence editing the
avant-garde journal *neue texte* and, with his wife Margret Bäcker, running the publishing house edition neue
texte. His papers in the Literary Archive of the Austrian
National Library contain hundreds of pages about the
principles behind his writing. He ultimately published
very little about his own work, just the few short texts collected in this volume, most of which appeared in Austrian
literary magazines. "On the Topography of Mauthausen,"
his longest theoretical text, was delivered as a lecture at an
academic conference on concentration camp memorials.
In unpublished notes, he laments his inability to theorize his writing, but also claims that quotational writing
requires no theorization—and that any theory would fall
short anyway.* He took on the task nonetheless, drawing

---

*   Heimrad Bäcker, untitled notes, Austrian National Library Literary Archive, Nachlaß Heimrad Bäcker, ÖLA 214/03, 29/149.

on his training as a philosopher; he wrote his 1953 doctoral dissertation in philosophy at the University of Vienna on the problem of communication and community, and his poetics evoke the German philosophical tradition. Gradually, though, philosophers' names disappear from his texts, even if philosophical concepts like the Hegelian "reflection" (or "reflexion"), *Aufhebung*, and historicity, as well as the phenomenological emphasis on the everyday and ordinariness, remain.

Bäcker's poetry and photography return again and again to the Shoah. *transcript* was followed by *transcript 2*, and *SEASCAPE* and *epitaph* covered the same material. The 1995 radio play *Gehen wir wirklich in den Tod?* (Are We Really Going to Die?) is based on *transcript*, and a stage version of *epitaph* was presented for the first time at the Hebbel Theater in Berlin in 1993. His theoretical texts often quote the same passages from his own work, which he explored from different angles at different times, and for this reason, the repetition of quotations is maintained in the essays translated here. He also photographed the same objects, buildings, and grounds in Mauthausen dozens of times, and when he was too frail to walk around the grounds, he began to photograph his television screen during broadcasts of documentaries about National Socialism and the Shoah. He made many prints of the same negatives, with particular attention to the neglected, looted, and decaying remnants of the quarries and industrial sites that could still be found in and around Mauthausen.

In the afterword to *epitaph*, Bäcker writes of his life's work as identical with his life, as an inconclusive attempt

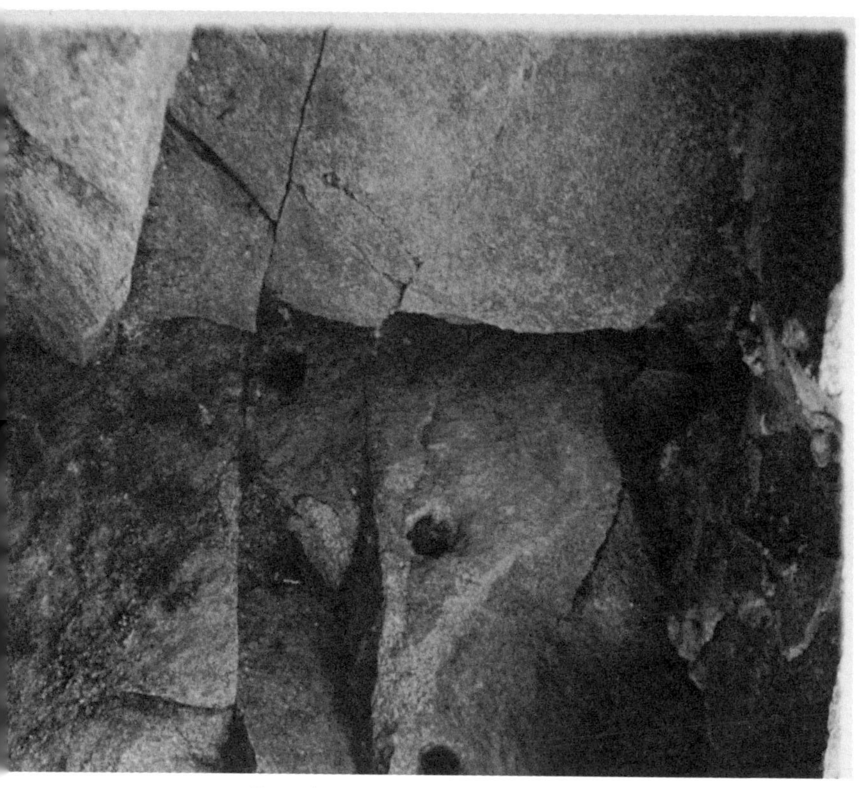

Traces of Labor in the Wiener Graben Quarry in the Mauthausen Concentration Camp

to come to terms with history and with his biography. His writing and photography aimed to be a "process of *Aufhebung*" or a "'negation of negation' (Jean Améry)" that he thought would "come to an end not with a single publication, but with the existence of its author." "Aufhebung" here means both overcoming and passing on in a new form, as poetry. Where others were able to move on, Bäcker singlemindedly pursued his examination of the Shoah for decades. He was aware of the repetitiveness of his work. As he writes in one of his unpublished notes, his "topic is not a topic," not one subject matter among others, and for this

reason, there was no way to "finish up."* Bäcker's poetry
and poetics transmit his sense of a permanent obligation to
develop methods for presenting and understanding history.

—Patrick Greaney, February 2024

---

*   Heimrad Bäcker, untitled notes, Austrian National Library Literary Archive, Nachlaß Heimrad Bäcker, ÖLA 214/03, 8/149.

DOCUMENTARY POETRY

DOCUMENTARY POETRY

At the beginning of temporality and historicity, at the beginning of history, Cain is asked where his brother Abel is. He responds with a question: "Am I my brother's keeper?" Mythology reveals a substitution at the beginning of time and history: the Cainian language convention. A category of good conduct, being someone's keeper, is used to conceal an action; in his denial, Cain clings to an ethical category and deploys it for something completely different.

Language from the cellars of history, the language of "Top Secret Matters of the Reich," is laden with relicts from the historical canon of good conduct, with concepts of versatile goodness. My brother's keeper becomes Heinrich Himmler, a man who "remains decent" as he has murder carried out on a grand scale. Language conventions, which even the lower ranks were made to follow, allow murder to become a "glorious chapter in German history." This style, laden with inherited humanistic ideals, forces one into speech acts that perform substitutions. Concepts remain intact as their reach is increased ad infinitum, while what can only be described with superlatives like *the most unbelievable* and *the most unimaginable* takes place in the caverns of the Third Reich.

National Socialism made use of an alphabet of continually recurring formulae, as in the pattern laid out by Reinhard Heydrich in his invitation to the Wannsee Conference, where the "implementation of the desired Final Solution to the Jewish Question" was set in motion:

in the interest of the achievement in particular

already through ongoing transports

about the preparatory measures all

necessary preparations

as a further option for a solution

of the same opinion

after appropriate prior approval

with this final solution

necessities related to social policies

whatever remnants might be left over

separating the sexes

with breakfast to follow

as the subject of a discussion

Am Großen Wannsee 56/58.

Actions are performed in the interest of a shared attitude; this gibberish (represented here as fragments) circulates in its own closed circuits as the realization of an unspoken intention (later, in Jerusalem, Eichmann said that the conference participants all knew exactly what the phrase "Final Solution" meant): language as an administrative act of violence, language that reproduces its own formulaic character and conceals victims and perpetrators. If I stick to this language, if I put it in writing in a book (and that means: if I expose it to reflection by using it just as it was used, but with literary intent), the relational structure in which it then appears, in a new system, enables it to be recognized as that which it does not want to be recognized as: a language of radical substitution. I negate its negation, and if this is successful, the result is the positioning of the text such that it reveals itself. Its linguistic shells are dissolved; the event is released from its mask made of ideals; its stance is clarified, and its structure becomes visible: as gibberish that plunders the arsenal of inherited concepts and skillfully uses them to seduce and go about its work. Helmut Heissenbüttel's poem "Germany 1944" was the first, the guiding text; it showed how substitutions can be undone and speech restored to its authentic dimensions, to its original pattern, by quotation, even if the original is barely distinguishable from its own copy.

The type of text known as a "document" becomes literature when a correspondence emerges among chosen parts of a text. In his essay on collage, Franz Mon refers to a peculiar relation that is also at work here: that which appears to be the furthest apart is what actually most belongs together, or, as Max Ernst puts it, "the juxtaposition of two (or more) seemingly distant realities" ignites "the most powerful poetic spark." Applied to our example: my book *transcript* brings together in its "system of relations" (Friedrich Achleitner) these realities that are essentially foreign to one another: the statistics in an insurance yearbook (with their fixed formulae of unadjusted values, the number of confirmed deaths, the number of deaths that conform to statistical models, the adjusted and unadjusted mortality probabilities) and that which cannot be grasped in any ordinary experience, murder on a scale beyond every mortality probability. Concepts cannot conceive of this, or if they can, then only within this textual system of "sparking" absurdity.

transcript and my radio play *Are We Really Going to Die?* could be called clustered collages. Unlike other collage forms, these texts quote continuously. The method is not new (except maybe for the fact that it takes on an extreme form). *Berlin Alexanderplatz* and *Danton's Death* come to mind: one fifth of Büchner's work consists of passages from court files or history books about the French Revolution. The historical-critical edition compares Büchner's text with the sources; they are almost identical; the straightforwardness of the diction is due to the quotations—a closer proximity is unimaginable.

What took place cannot be captured with the literary forms developed on this side of the terror. And yet a method must be found (one doesn't have a choice) that is adequate to its negative monumentality.

The "topic" here is a language whose signs are also available to Odilo Globocnik in his report to Himmler on Operation Reinhard (which included the killing centers Belzec, Sobibor, Treblinka). The topic is not the report or Operation Reinhard itself, but rather a language that is capable of presenting the operation and its results. It is colloquial language, everyday language, bureaucratic language, a language of ideals (and their perversion), a language for giving orders, and for statistics. The report on Operation Reinhard uses familiar speech patterns. Since, however, this is a special case, since this is not a report like any other, but rather the conclusion of a killing operation on a grand scale, its language (its calculations, to the penny, of the value of confiscated clothing, jewelry, and currency) is laden with the weight of what occurred: its language refers to the contents that it transports. I am faced with the problem that language is capable of formulating and transporting the unimaginable in a completely normal style.

When I quote documents, there is no literariness beyond the quotation (except the serialization, repetition, omission; except the *transcript* system): here lies the difference from narrative, from poetic subjectivity, from the stage of a radio play, etc. In a quotation, subjectivity (perpetrators' and victims') can manifest itself without being refracted by literature. The author's reflection on the quotation takes place in the act of quoting. The body of the word fills itself up as it takes back into itself what was once said.

Documentary literature cuts through the skeins of imagination, paralyzes the literary impulses of the will, makes secondary reflection into an unnecessary addition, and negates remembrance ceremonies' formulaic horror; repeated use does not wear it down, and it makes visible that which is hidden by public and private mediocrity and its schematizing tendencies.

The literature of quotation as a literature of identity with non-literary reality (or its appearance), which is itself an accumulation, an immense patchwork of quotations. The author surgically removes them from a reality in flux, and if this is successful, they lose nothing of their authenticity.

When a document is ripped out of its isolation and forced into the isolation created by a formal principle, it acquires a new efficacy. Identity of document and literature. Documents are literature that writes itself and is recognized as literature. Isolation, abbreviation, spatial positioning, sequencing, removal of capital letters merely render visible what the document already contains as description, report, statistics.

1. those who speak.

2. those who speak in the transcript *system.*

A phenomenon constitutes its counterphenomenon. Dialectic of pain and statistics.

(1992)

MIRRORING

1.

On April 13, 1961, Hannah Arendt writes from Jerusalem, where she is covering the Eichmann Trial, to her teacher and friend Karl Jaspers: Eichmann is "like a ghost, losing substance by the minute." And years later, her final work, *The Life of the Mind*, written shortly before her death, opens with reflections on how evil manifested in Eichmann as "quite ordinary, average, and neither demonic nor monstrous," not even grounded in ideology.

"The normal patterns of modern, rational action … bear within themselves a potential that was dramatically revealed in the Holocaust" (Zygmunt Bauman). If one of the characteristics of a civilization is the production of moral indifference, then orders authorized from above and an entrenched operational routine are all that is needed to eliminate a population previously made into chosen victims by methodical dehumanizing measures (Bauman/Kelman).

With the concept of the banality of evil, H.A. reverses previous hermeneutic models of violence, turning them away from the exemplary and the numinous, from the biologically predisposed and inevitable, and back toward average human beings as potential perpetrators.

She relieved us of the burden of evil as a grand substantialized magnitude and also taught that, as a result, the *vita activa* is capable of finding the means to act against evil understood in its everydayness, as long as the required imperative to *"stop* and think" (H.A.) is heeded: this thinking attentiveness is a form of Jaspers's communication, which is—according to his excessive formulation— "the all-embracing essence of humanity" that makes community possible. Communication's mode of existence is annulled when the Arendtian stop-and-think is eliminated in favor of banal functioning within the habitual categories of commanding and obeying, in which there is not even the will to evil, just the rational solution to given problems.

The banality of evil is mirrored in the banality of formulaic expressions for death. They are recorded in orders, statistics, train schedules, in the daily reports, letters, and implementation notifications about the banally normal implementation of actions understood normally. Quotation: "I was only tasked with carrying out the killing." No intensification (or accusation or condemnation) through elements external to the documents is necessary. What occurred articulates itself in what became part of the record:

> in the interest of the achievement in particular
> already through ongoing transports
> about the preparatory measures all
> necessary preparations
> as a further option for a solution
> of the same opinion
> after appropriate prior approval
> with this final solution
> necessities related to social policies
> whatever remnants might be left over
> separating the sexes

with breakfast to follow
as the subject of a discussion
Am Großen Wannsee 56/58.

As an author, I take on the task of opening up this material. Having succumb in my youth to banal sloganeering, I present it using the methods of *transcript* (whose formalist approaches allow what happened to come to the fore even more clearly). No matter how many years ago it happened, it still has an acute presence in the documents.

2.

The alphabet of German fascism is composed of words of death. But the words of death speak not of death, rather of BEING EMIGRATED / of PROCESSING / of PACIFICATION CAMPAIGNS / of PURIFICATION / of DISINFECTION / of DISINFESTATION / of TOTAL YIELDS / of LARGE MOBILIZATIONS / of PREPARING THE JEWS / of J-CAMPAIGNS / of J-TRANSPORTS / of the DEPORTATION OF CHILDREN / of RESTORING THE PEACE / of SPECIAL TRAIN SERVICE / of SPECIAL ACCOMMODATIONS / of ST or SPECIAL TREATMENT / of GV or GASSING VEHICLES, and have to do with the fact that the act of LOADING CARGO leads to the doors of the gas vans.

3.

There are written records that make forms available: the
form of a letter, of a numeral, of a sound combination, of
an abbreviation, of a line's length, of an ordering of lines,
of addition signs, of the notes a) b) c), of the superscript 3,
of the doubling of the same within a divided German and
Polish placard text, of the increasing number of transport
trains, of the decreasing number of the living, the not-yet-
killed, of the ditto mark, one for each person killed, of the
repeated time of day given for when a life ends in death,
of the points one through four, after which a judgment is
made: history's appendix.

In documents, I come across: rudimentary concrete
and concrete-visual texts that can be decoded in a pro-
gressive process of concretion. A literary construction can
be developed out of a bureaucratic note's unintentionally
potent organizational rituals. Documentary language patterns—which only appear not to be appropriate for what
they refer to—are characterized by an explosive literary
force. As an author, I am caught up in their current and can
only resist by fixing them in a new, formally determined
system. Material, with history attached to it, becomes an
element in a language pattern detached from its immediate cause, from the moment, from the event, a pattern
that results from opening up everyday texts otherwise
relegated to the history of ideas, historical studies, crimi-
nology, etc., and whose structural aspect goes unnoticed.
If we take a closer look at them, it is easy to break through
the barrier of everyday language and make visible the ge-
ometry of the text. What someone just casually says can be

concretized. This is what I try to do, and this is what makes me a concrete author, one who perceives the possibility of concretion in what has been passed down as documents. Sometimes that occurs in a 1:1 process (with elements that completely coincide, document=text), sometimes through reduction, repetition, montage, seriality.

The detection of fallow linguistic material has a formal intention; it does not moralize, assign blame, justify. If a set form is found in documents and excised, the result exceeds the particular detail. This also applies to statistics when they are inserted into a system not characterized by its reporting of numbers, but by their reflection as literature: literature as the possibility of declaring even apparently nonliterary elements to be literature.

(1994)

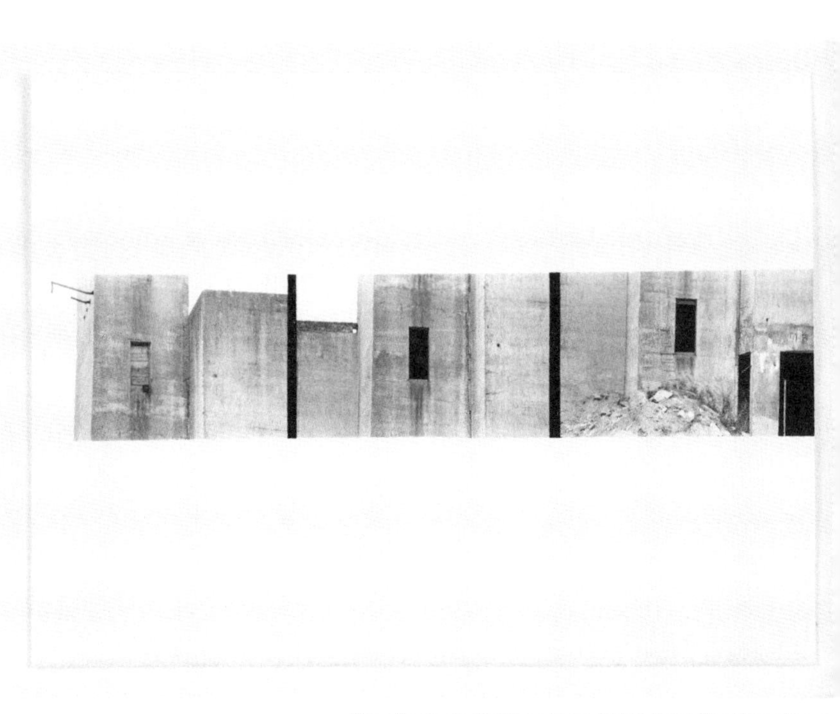

Stone Crusher in the Gusen Concentration Camp (Condition after 19

ON THE TOPOGRAPHY OF MAUTHAUSEN
LECTURE DELIVERED AT THE CONFERENCE "THE ASSAULT OF THE PRESENT ON THE PAST"

1.

If you take the road running northwest from the town of Mauthausen to the concentration camp, you will notice the remnants of complex facilities overgrown with vegetation: foundations, massive perimeter walls, low walls with anchor bars, tower-like masses of concrete. In the immediate environs of the camp quarry called the *Wiener Graben* (Vienna Dig), evidence from the era has been preserved: fragments of the buildings drawn in the plan for the site's construction like the stone crusher, the Great Hall, cable mechanisms, watchhouses. All the useful structures, all the easily removable wood and masonry disappeared long ago. Their removal went on for decades and continues to this day. The reason: a failure to incorporate into the protected museum area all the industrial buildings used for stone extraction and processing. On many occasions, I have pointed out the general indifference toward these historical grounds, but in the end the financial argument has always won out: it would be too expensive to acquire this or that plot of land and make it into part of the Mauthausen Concentration Camp Museum. A stone's throw from the Wiener Graben's north entrance, a new act of violence is taking place right now: a plumbing company is leveling out the terrain of the so-called Great Hall, the outdoor gathering area for prisoners. The northern part has already been buried, covered with excavated material and pipes—so, in 1995 and 1996, in front of our very eyes, they have been allowed to go against the October 1994 recommendation of the International Advisory Commission on the Mauthausen Concentration Camp Memorial, whose memorandum calls for parcels of land to be bought in order to secure architectural remnants in the main camp, the neighboring Gusen camp, and the satellite camps, and in order to prevent the terrain around the camp from being built up; this is particularly important, the memorandum said.[*]

How easy it would have been to trace the wartime paths that led to the remnants of work areas, and to indicate with signs how the terrain was used. That did not happen. So all that remains are relicts exposed to time. Their form of existence is mere presence-at-hand, without use or history, and nothing else. The Great Hall, the two quarries (Wiener Graben and Gusen) exist outside of the history that once determined what they were.

When a historical object becomes part of our sense of museal classification, the process often whitewashes, smooths out, aestheticizes. To give an example: the only street still present in the camp, which was also the *Appellplatz* where roll call was taken, was completely asphalted over—a major alteration of its original condition. Or: in the early 1970s, I photographed (as Erich Hartmann already had in 1961) one of the camp's towers, as well as a wall running perpendicular to the camp's southern side, and then one day they were no longer there. They had to give

---

[*] Vorschläge der Sachverständigenkommission zur Gedenkstätte Konzentrationslager Mauthausen, *zeitgeschichte* 9/10 (1995): 357–71.

way to an expansion of the parking lot; an easily managed site and convenient access to the memorial buildings were the deciding factors.

An argument can always be made to justify the manipulation of historical grounds, but they, along with any reconstructions, should be clearly indicated, which they have not been in Mauthausen (an egregious example is the gas chamber's shoddy, inaccurate restoration). Nowhere is it stated that the Prayer Room (the Chapel) did not exist between 1938 and 1945, but was built into the laundry barrack later—which used up most of the Federal Government's first subvention payment for the camp renovation. This added construction gives too much weight to Catholicism and too little consideration to other faiths; many prisoners belonged to other faiths or were not religious, as is true of visitors today.

In the post-war years, many buildings were removed, and barracks were sold for living quarters, torn down, or let go to ruin. Immediately after the war, the town of Mauthausen used the housing-shortage argument to buy up the barracks, and a great deal of material and original equipment was also removed by freed prisoners (especially Czech prisoners, who were favored by the American troops who took over the camp). Hans Maršálek, the camp's historian, speaks of five tons of material that disappeared into Czechoslovakia. Recently, Austrian researchers made an important find: the exhaust fan from the Mauthausen gas chamber was located in the museum of the Terezín/Theresienstadt Memorial. After the Allied occupation zones were defined, the camp was also used by Russian troops, who generously helped themselves, and then, after their withdrawal, it was left unattended for more than a year, accessible to everyone. All that remained after that were four barracks and a few stone buildings, meager relicts without window frames, electrical wiring, heating systems, wooden structures, doorknobs, signs, etc. There was also interest in the stones used for the exterior walls and the large stones with numbers for the barracks on them, so in the end even the enclosure wall around the infamous Barrack 20, the barrack for the Russian prisoners of "Aktion K" ("The Bullet Campaign") disappeared.

If our conference topic, "The Assault of the Present on the Past," is taken in a limited, direct way, then these losses can also be registered as crass theft. Hasty, ceaseless restoration is undertaken in an attempt to make up for them. The camp's appearance today, with its flawless external walls, a few flawlessly preserved barracks, the stone buildings, and the flawlessly restored "Death Stairs"—what a conceptual pair, flawless and Death Stairs—herein lies the irony. Meanwhile, the Appellplatz of Mauthausen's twin camp, Gusen, preserved intact until two years ago, was handed over to the owner of a mushroom-growing company, which just recently erected fences and bars to block access; the eastern enclosure wall, which is still standing, was also included, and even the camp's gate house was renovated and turned into a residential villa. The ensemble (to use a preservationists' term) of the Appellplatz—the enclosure wall, gate house, and stone crusher—was destroyed.

Topographical changes like this do not seem to particularly bother the museum administrators in their section of the Austrian Ministry of the Interior. There are, however, those who have taken it upon themselves to rectify

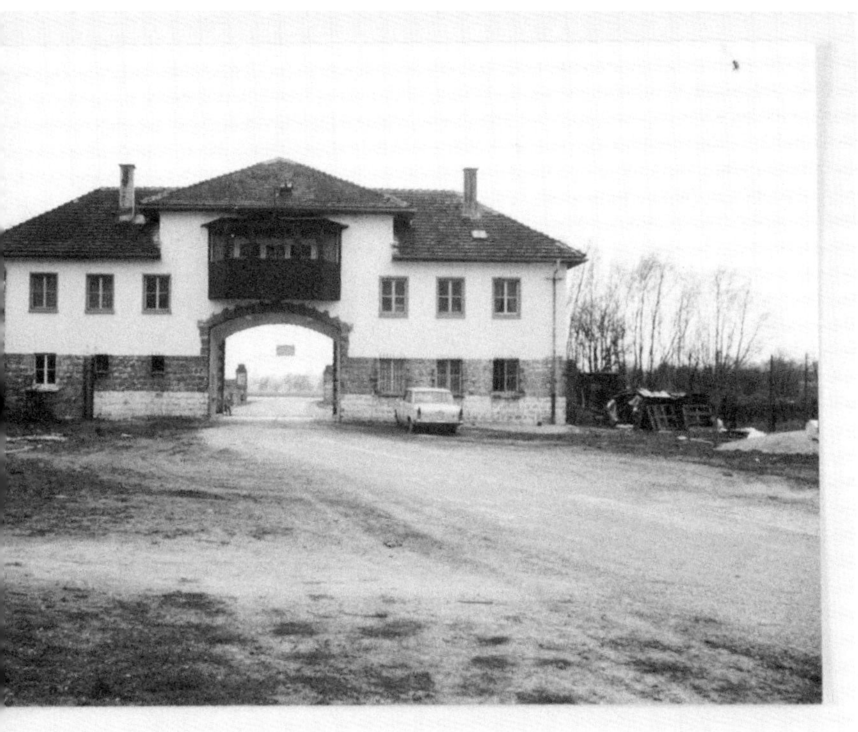

Gatehouse to the Gusen Concentration Camp (Condition 1945-1993)

these long-recognized shortcomings and who do not accept historical losses without protest; for years, they have been fighting a battle against bureaucratic indifference, to no avail. In particular, the members of the Institute for Contemporary History at the University of Vienna (Florian Freund, Bertrand Perz, and Karl Stuhlpfarrer) have drawn on the latest professional developments in their field to lay the groundwork for change. But as the example of the renovated gatehouse shows, there are limits to what they can do. According to the Advisory Commission's 1994 expert opinion, "The prompt securing of structural remains at the former concentration camp of Gusen is

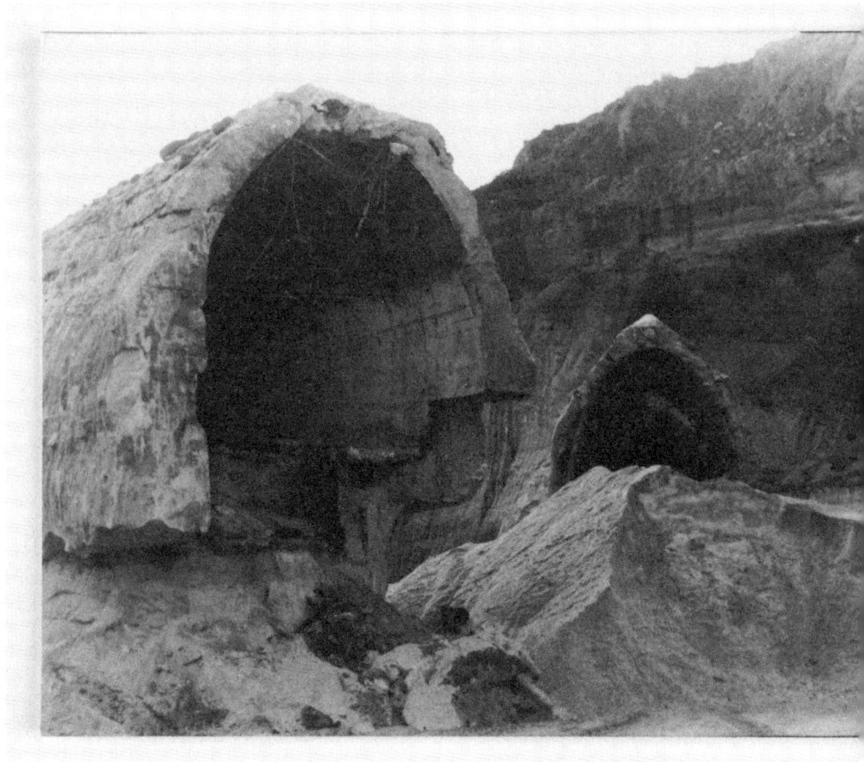

Tunnels of "Rock Crystal," Underground Factory for Production of Me 262 Jet Fighter,
in St. Georgen (Concentration Camp Mauthausen/Gusen II)

urgent, in order to forestall further destruction of key components such as the so-called *Jourhaus*, or gatehouse, or of the gravel crusher, which is a central landmark of the Gusen memorial."

As this was being said, the destruction was already underway. As you probably know, the Gusen camp played a crucial part in the production of DEST, Deutsche Erd- und Steinwerke GmbH (the German Earth & Stone Works Company), which was owned by the SS. In three of their quarries, granite was extracted. Weapons and aviation parts were produced there in factories owned by the Messerschmidt and Steyr companies. So were fuselage and wing components for the Me 262 jet fighter, which were made as part of the so-called "Kammler Program" in underground tunnels in the Gusen II/St. Georgen camp, which were dug out in an incomparably murderous deployment of slave labor. These underground witnesses, the extensive tunnel systems, are no longer safe from the grasp of industry, since they stand in the way of the extraction of sand. Tunnels G1 and O1 have already been demolished.*

---

* Hans Marsalek, *Gusen: Kurze dokumentarische Geschichte eines Nebenlagers des-KZ Mauthausen* (Vienna: Bauers, 1968); Rudolf A. Haunschmied, "1938/1945: Zum Gedenken," in *300 Jahre erweitertes Marktrecht St. Georgen a.d. Gusen* (St. Georgen an der Gusen: Marktgemeinde St. Georgen an der Gusen, 1989), 74–109.

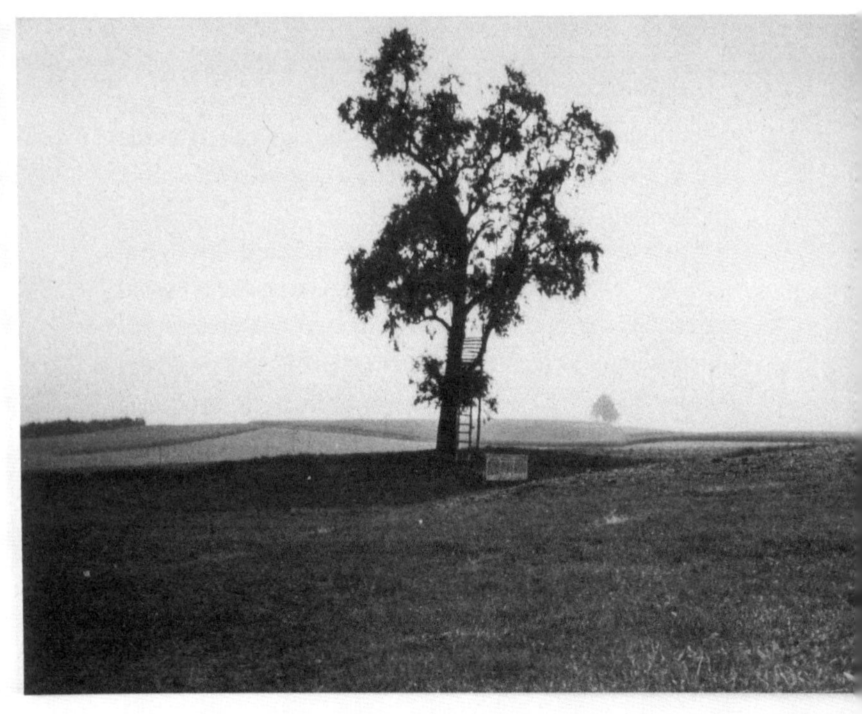

Memorial Marker Mauthausen Concentration Camp 1968

2.

Landscape, terrain, geography are interpreted by memorial stones. Here, there is a field, a tree, a hilly horizon, elements of space that we find ourselves in as historical beings. The stone and the inscription in the stone have to do with that. Up against a small elevation, a stone stands under a tree used as a hunting blind. This photo is from 1968 (my first roll of film from Mauthausen). In the meantime, the scenery has changed. The tree is gone, the lightly raised hill it stood on has been gradually worn down by planting, as has the path once taken by the occasional visitor who made their way to the memorial stone, the northernmost point of the Mauthausen complex. In the surrounding areas, there is terrain used for farming and no longer used for killing; the execution site to the right has been leveled out; in the fall, cows are put out to pasture here.

The particular untouched aspect of the unmoved stone, its gathered historicity (or, to be more exact: the human historicity gathered and present in it) imparts itself, makes this or that state of the landscape (the one from 1968 or from 1995) into states that exist in relation to this spot, where our historicity culminated in violence.

This stone has concrete presence. It is not a symbol, but a concretion. In it, historical events congeal into a simple formula; perhaps this is also because it breaks through other memorial stones' pathos-laden gestures, and we who come upon it can let ourselves hear its simple speech.

In the Mauthausen Memorial Park, there are few inscriptions that are moving, touching. They are not to be

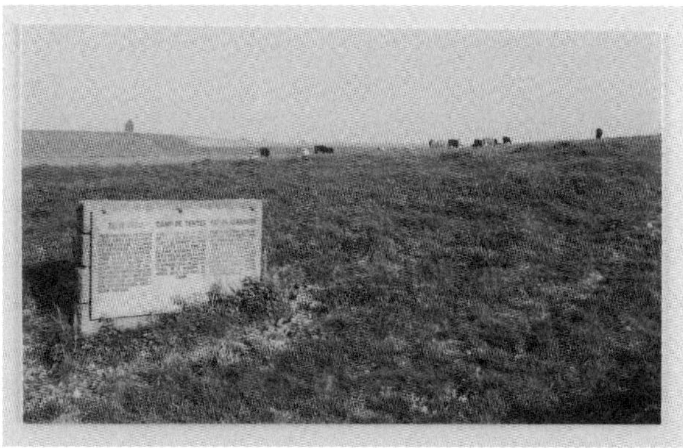

Memorial Marker Mauthausen Concentration Camp 1995

found on the large, heroic national memorials, but on the private remembrance plaques. Unfortunately, these are more exposed to the elements and not as durable, nor are they massive constructions. The memorial site's administration has failed to perform occasional or even annual maintenance—to repair the damage to these memorial plaques donated by family members or hometowns and to reattach or replace letters or reassemble plaques and medallions that have fallen apart, let alone archive them. Some memorial stones lie abandoned in the terrain around the camp; suddenly one comes upon the name of a victim— Eugène Maurice Le Corre, April 21, 1898–May 2, 1945—in the tall grass, among plaques fallen into disrepair.

The emptied-out quarry intensifies the negative image of this way of dealing with history. All the blocks of stone that can still be seen in a photo from the early 1970s, blocks which were cut out by prisoners (since 1945, the quarry has been idle), stone whose weight caused hundreds upon hundreds to perish on the Death Stairs (historical sources verify this): they were removed and presumably sold at a profit (this issue is discussed by historians in an expert opinion commissioned by the Federal Chancellery). What happened on these stairs was described on May 10, 1945, right after the camp's liberation, by Richard Dietl, a member of the communist resistance from the town of Wels. He was the only survivor from his group. I believe that this unknown description belongs to the Mauthausen topography just as much as the stairs themselves: "Höllermann stood at the top of the stairs, covered in blood. I saw for myself, this is the truth, two SS men were beating him and throwing him up against the fence, where two SS watchmen

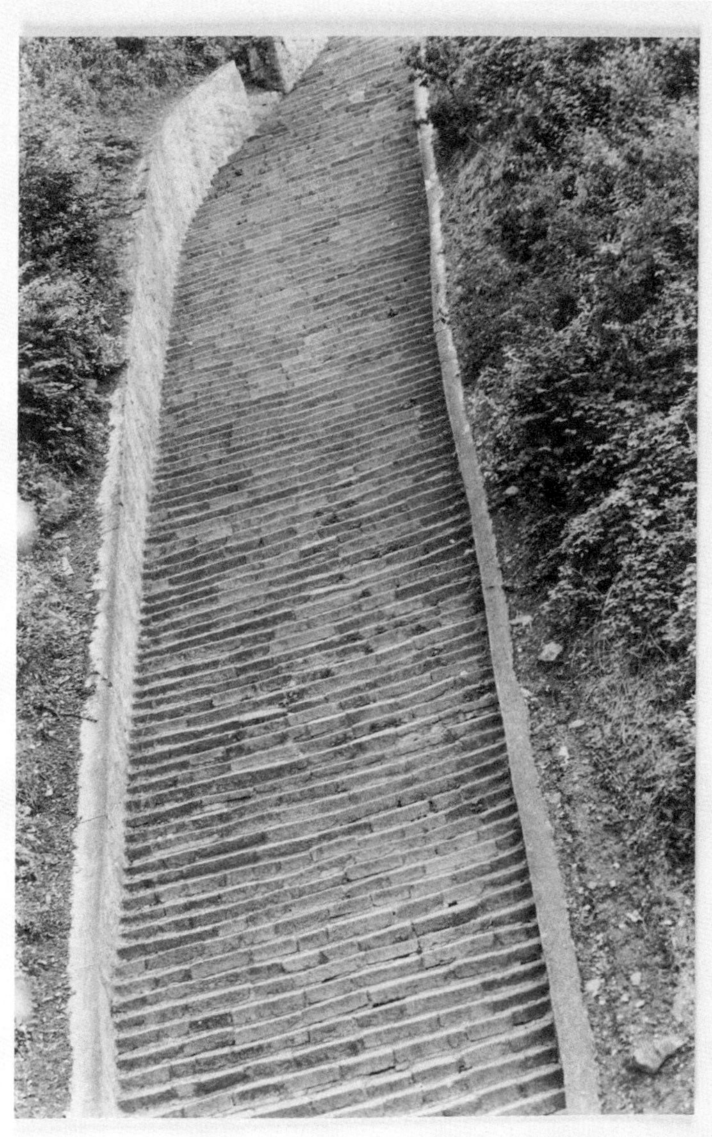

"Death Stairs" in the Wiener Graben Quarry of the Mauthausen Concentration Camp

were waiting with their rifles and put an end to his life with two shots. Schwarzlmüller and Fritz Alois were next, they came up to me pleading: 'Richard, you still have enough strength, you have to make it, send my best to my wife and children, if you're able to bear this. We know we have to die now, our strength is at an end.' With tears in our eyes, we bade each other farewell, I heard three shots and I knew who they were for. Below, at the bottom of the stairs, Ernst Stadler was lying there, just as bad off as all of us. I tried to go over to him, and he was only able to say to me, 'Richard, I can't do it anymore'; he tried to reach his hand out to me, but it got beaten out of the way, and I got a blow to the head. When I climbed the stairs for the third time with Sepp Teufel, carrying the required weight of stone, Ernst had already been shot dead. Five times we climbed those 187 stairs, and at the end of the first day, I realized that nine good comrades had been shot dead."*

3.

Most texts in my linguistic topography of Mauthausen came about through repeated study of Hans Maršálek's book *The History of the Mauthausen Concentration Camp*.** Their

---

*   Dokumentationsarchiv des österreichischen Widerstandes, *Widerstand und Verfolgung in Oberösterreich 1934-1945* (Vienna: Österreichischer Bundesverlag, 1982), 2:585.

** Hans Marsalek, *Die Geschichte des Konzentrationslagers Mauthausen* (Vienna: Österreichische Lagergemeinschaft Mauthausen, 1980).

method: serialization, repetition, enumeration, omission, or simple reproduction via quotations.

An example: On May 26, 1943, the order was issued by Himmler to all the concentration camps' commands: to conceal the numbers of the dead, consecutive counting would no longer be allowed, but instead deaths would be counted as Roman numeral I/1–185, then the count would start again with Roman numeral II/1–185, then Roman numeral III/1–185, etc. At the beginning of the year, counting would be turned back to Roman numeral I/1–185.

These instructions produced the material for two documentary texts: first, for a circular text using the abbreviations for concentration camp names from the top of Himmler's letter: Dachau, Sachsenhausen, Buchenwald, Mauthausen, Flossenbürg, etc., that is: Da., Sa., Bu., Mau., Flo. These abbreviations were listed under the usual "Re:" heading. Second, for a linguistic concretion of the concealment, that is, the cover-up of the number of dead.

Both texts do more than merely follow formal processes, as if there were no correspondence with reality beyond permutation and enumeration. The circular list Da., Sa., Bu., Mau., Flo., Au. points to the circulation of prisoners, who, as we know, were often sent from camp to camp, according to needs expressed by camp commandants, or by the Reich Security Main Office or Oswald Pohl's SS Main Economic and Administrative Office, which oversaw all the camps. There were transports when labor power was needed, when new camps were founded, when supply had to make up for killings or deaths, not to mention the transports for evacuations. The formal circulation reflects and draws attention to the circulating flow of prisoners from camp to camp.

Da., Sah., Bu., Mau., Flo., Neu., Au., GrRo., Natz., Nie., Stu., Lub., Rav., Herz.
Sah., Bu., Mau., Flo., Neu., Au., GrRo., Natz., Nie., Stu., Lub., Rav., Herz., Da.
Bu., Mau., Flo., Neu., Au., GrRo., Natz., Nie., Stu., Lub., Rav., Herz., Da., Sah.
Mau., Flo., Neu., Au., GrRo., Natz., Nie., Stu., Lub., Rav., Herz., Da., Sah., Bu.
Flo., Neu., Au., GrRo., Natz., Nie., Stu., Lub., Rav., Herz., Da., Sah., Bu., Mau.
Neu., Au., GrRo., Natz., Nie., Stu., Lub., Rav., Herz., Da., Sah., Bu., Mau., Flo.
Au., GrRo., Natz., Nie., Stu., Lub., Rav., Herz., Da., Sah., Bu., Mau., Flo., Neu.
GrRo., Natz., Nie., Stu., Lub., Rav., Herz., Da., Sah., Bu., Mau., Flo., Neu., Au.
Natz., Nie., Stu., Lub., Rav., Herz., Da., Sah., Bu., Mau., Flo., Neu., Au., GrRo.
Nie., Stu., Lub., Rav., Herz., Da., Sah., Bu., Mau., Flo., Neu., Au., GrRo., Natz.
Stu., Lub., Rav., Herz., Da., Sah., Bu., Mau., Flo., Neu., Au., GrRo., Natz., Nie.
Lub., Rav., Herz., Da., Sah., Bu., Mau., Flo., Neu., Au., GrRo., Natz., Nie., Stu.
Rav., Herz., Da., Sah., Bu., Mau., Flo., Neu., Au., GrRo., Natz., Nie., Stu., Lub.
Herz., Da., Sah., Bu., Mau., Flo., Neu., Au., GrRo., Natz., Nie., Stu., Lub., Rav.

The second text takes seriously Himmler's methodical instructions about veiling conditions in the camps through a veiled way of counting the dead. From reports by women prisoners who worked in Auschwitz's administration, we happen to know that this was indeed how the count was kept, albeit in Auschwitz only up to 180, out of whatever intention or memory lapse.

I/1 I/2 I/3 I/4 I/5 I/6 I/7 I/8 I/9 I/10 I/11 I/12 I/13 I/14 I/15 I/16 I/17 I/18 I/19 I/20 I/21 I/22 I/23 I/24 I/25 I/26 I/27 I/28 I/29 I/30 I/31 I/32 I/33 I/34 I/35 I/36 I/37 I/38 I/39 I/40 I/41 I/42 I/43 I/44 I/45 I/46 I/47 I/48 I/49 I/50 I/51 I/52 I/53 I/54 I/55 I/56 I/57 I/58 I/59 I/60 I/61 I/62 I/63 I/64 I/65 I/66 I/67 I/68 I/69 I/70 I/71 I/72 I/73 I/74 I/75 I/76 I/77

I/78 I/79 I/80 I/81 I/82 I/83 I/84 I/85 I/86 I/87 I/88 I/89 I/90 I/91 I/92 I/93 I/94 I/95 I/96 I/97 I/98 I/99 I/100 I/101 I/102 I/103 I/104 I/105 I/106 I/107 I/108 I/109 I/110 I/111 I/112 I/113 I/114 I/115 I/116 I/117 I/118 I/119 I/120 I/121 I/122 I/123 I/124 I/125 I/126 I/127 I/128 I/129 I/130 I/131 I/132 I/133 I/134 I/135 I/136 I/137 I/138 I/139 I/140 I/141 I/142 I/143 I/144 I/145 I/146 I/147 I/148 I/149 I/150 I/151 I/152 I/153 I/154 I/155 I/156 I/157 I/158 I/159 I/160 I/161 I/162 I/163 I/164 I/165 I/166 I/167 I/168 I/169 I/170 I/171 I/172 I/173 I/174 I/175 I/176 I/177 I/178 I/179 I/180 I/181 I/182 I/183 I/184 I/185 II/1 II/2 II/3 II/4 II/5 II/6 II/7 II/8 II/9 II/10 II/11 II/12 II/13 II/14 II/15 II/16 II/17 II/18 II/19 II/20 II/21 II/22 II/23 II/24 II/25 II/26 II/27 II/28 II/29 II/30 II/31 II/32 II/33 II/34 II/35 II/36 II/37 II/38 II/39 II/40 II/41 II/42 II/43 II/44 II/45 II/46 II/47 II/48 II/49 II/50 II/51 II/52 II/53 II/54 II/55 II/56 II/57 II/58 II/59 II/60 II/61 II/62 II/63 II/64 II/65 II/66 II/67 II/68 II/69 II/70 II/71 II/72 II/73 II/74 II/75 II/76 II/77 II/78 II/79 II/80 II/81 II/82 II/83 II/84 II/85 II/86 II/87 II/88 II/89 II/90 II/91 II/92 II/93 II/94 II/95 II/96 II/97 II/98 II/99 II/100 II/101 II/102 II/103 II/104 II/105 II/106 II/107 II/108 II/109 II/110 II/111 II/112 II/113 II/114 II/115 II/116 II/117 II/118 II/119 II/120 II/121 II/122 II/123 II/124 II/125 II/126 II/127 II/128 II/129 II/130 II/131 II/132 II/133 II/134 II/135 II/136 II/137 II/138 II/139 II/140 II/141 II/142 II/143 II/144 II/145 II/146 II/147 II/148 II/149 II/150 II/151 II/152 II/153 II/154 II/155 II/156 II/157 II/158 II/159 II/160 II/161 II/162 II/163 II/164 II/165 II/166 II/167 II/168 II/169 II/170 II/171 II/172 II/173 II/174 II/175 II/176 II/177 II/178 II/179 II/180 II/181 II/182 II/183 II/184 II/185 III/1 III/2 III/3 III/4 III/5 III/6 III/7 III/8 III/9 III/10 III/11 III/12 III/13 III/14 III/15 III/16 III/17 III/18 III/19 III/20 III/21 III/22 III/23 III/24 III/25 III/26 III/27 III/28 III/29 III/30 III/31 III/32 III/33 III/34 III/35 III/36 III/37 III/38 III/39 III/40 III/41 III/42 III/43 III/44 III/45 III/46 III/47 III/48 III/49 III/50 III/51 III/52 III/53 III/54 III/55 III/56 III/57 III/58 III/59 III/60 III/61 III/62 III/63 III/64 III/65 III/66 III/67 III/68 III/69 III/70 III/71 III/72 III/73 III/74 III/75 III/76 III/77

III/78 III/79 III/80 III/81 III/82 III/83 III/84 III/85 III/86 III/87 III/88
III/89 III/90 III/91 III/92 III/93 III/94 III/95 III/96 III/97 III/98 III/99
III/100 III/101 III/102 III/103 III/104 III/105 III/106 III/107 III/108
III/109 III/110 III/111 III/112 III/113 III/114 III/115 III/116 III/117 III/118
III/119 III/120 III/121 III/122 III/123 III/124 III/125 III/126 III/127 III/128
III/129 III/130 III/131 III/132 III/133 III/134 III/135 III/136 III/137 III/138
III/139 III/140 III/141 III/142 III/143 III/144 III/145 III/146 III/147
III/148 III/149 III/150 III/151 III/152 III/153 III/154 III/155 III/156
III/157 III/158 III/159 III/160 III/161 III/162 III/163 III/164 III/165 III/166
III/167 III/168 III/169 III/170 III/171 III/172 III/173 III/174 III/175 III/176
III/177 III/178 III/179 III/180 III/181 III/182 III/183 III/184 III/185 IV/1
IV/2 IV/3 IV/4 IV/5 IV/6 IV/7 IV/8 IV/9 IV/10 IV/11 IV/12 IV/13 IV/14
IV/15 IV/16 IV/17 IV/18 IV/19 IV/20 IV/21 IV/22 IV/23 IV/24 IV/25 IV/26
IV/27 IV/28 IV/29 IV/30 IV/31 IV/32 IV/33 IV/34 IV/35 IV/36 IV/37 IV/38
IV/39 IV/40 IV/41 IV/42 IV/43 IV/44 IV/45 IV/46 IV/47 IV/48 IV/49
IV/50 IV/51 IV/52 IV/53 IV/54 IV/55 IV/56 IV/57 IV/58 IV/59 IV/60 IV/61
IV/62 IV/63 IV/64 IV/65 IV/66 IV/67 IV/68 IV/69 IV/70 IV/71 IV/72 IV/73
IV/74 IV/75 IV/76 IV/77 IV/78 IV/79 IV/80 IV/81 IV/82 IV/83 IV/84
IV/85 IV/86 IV/87 IV/88 IV/89 IV/90 IV/91 IV/92 IV/93 IV/94 IV/95
IV/96 IV/97 IV/98 IV/99 IV/100 IV/101 IV/102 IV/103 IV/104 IV/105
IV/106 IV/107 IV/108 IV/109 IV/110 IV/111 IV/112 IV/113 IV/114 IV/115
IV/116 IV/117 IV/118 IV/119 IV/120 IV/121 IV/122 IV/123 IV/124 IV/125
IV/126 IV/127 IV/128 IV/129 IV/130 IV/131 IV/132 IV/133 IV/134 IV/135
IV/136 IV/137 IV/138 IV/139 IV/140 IV/141 IV/142 IV/143 IV/144 IV/145
IV/146 IV/147 IV/148 IV/149 IV/150 IV/151 IV/152 IV/153 IV/154 IV/155
IV/156 IV/157 IV/158 IV/159 IV/160 IV/161 IV/162 IV/163 IV/164 IV/165
IV/166 IV/167 IV/168 IV/169 IV/170 IV/171 IV/172 IV/173 IV/174 IV/175
IV/176 IV/177 IV/178 IV/179 IV/180 IV/181 IV/182 IV/183 IV/184 IV/185
in this way the respective number of cases of death that occur in a given
year are not made apparent

So if I continue to count with Roman numerals up to ten or fourteen or twenty-four (which always means that number times 185), there emerges, from Roman numeral to Roman numeral and back down to one again, an enormous field of the dead created by Himmler and not by the transcribing author, who just makes everything concrete and thus also visible in its full dimensions. These two texts serve as first examples of a literature bound to the *lingua tertii imperii*. If this language is taken seriously as an aesthetic phenomenon, a meta-aesthetic scenery quickly opens up.

Using the differentiation made by Droysen and Hoffmann, the death books of the Mauthausen concentration camp are monuments *from* the era; my concrete texts are memorials *to* the era. They are extracted from materials in those death books, materials from the era, the daily entries about what happened. This is the densest site, the nexus, where statistics and the methodical text extracted from them coincide, where writing from that time becomes—by means of *transcript*, by means of a form that comes afterward, that goes after its object—writing in memorial to that time.* Since no word is changed or invented, since nothing is fiction, these rows, these sentences spoken as repetition, these litanies with repeating typographical images, are documentary in nature. I also wrote out, as similar phrases repeating one after the other, the murders of Mauthausen inmates registered as part of Operation 14f13, the last phase of the "euthanasia" campaign; I wrote the dates and number of inmates, along with their transports' destination,

____

* Heimrad Bäcker, *transcript*, trans. Patrick Greaney and Vincent Kling (Champaign, IL: Dalkey Archive Press, 2010).

the Hartheim Euthanasia Center outside of Linz, from just one month in 1944. There emerged an austere series of recurring particles, a litany-like flow not of adoration, but of murder, which has nothing to do with prayer, but with the banally satanic, whose satanism is repeated like lines of statistics. This is the running text:

> 7.1 16 inmates reported "deceased" in hartheim / 7.3 25 inmates reported "deceased" in hartheim / 7.4 13 inmates reported "deceased" in hartheim / 7.5 33 inmates reported "deceased" in hartheim / 7.6 12 inmates reported "deceased" in hartheim / 7.7 14 inmates reported "deceased" in hartheim

In the Mauthausen death books, under the heading "Cause of death" on May 10, 1942, there is the notation: "execution per decree of the Security Police and Security Service of 4/30/1942." There then follows (after twenty-four inmates executed at other times) the entry "0:15 0:15 0:15 0:15 0:15 0:15" repeated 208 times, which means that a fictive time of day was entered for all these deaths instead of the actual time. Since the Mauthausen gas chamber held around 70 people, as we know from testimony by defendants before the Hagen District Court, these murders had to have taken place at three different points in time, at the least.* Should one say: for simplicity's sake, and then add: out of an indifferent sense of routine, the time was just noted as 0:15. As a reader of the documents of the Nuremberg Trials,

---

* Florian Freund, Bertrand Petz, Karl Stuhlpfarrer, "Historische Überreste von Tötungseinrichtungen im KZ Mauthausen," *zeitgeschichte* 9/10 (1995): 297–317.

I come upon the reprinting, in volume XXVI, of the death book, in paragraph form, and under the heading "Time of Death," the fixed entry 0:15 in a vertical column, one after the other. I realize the possibility of a concrete form by isolating the column and repeating it without any alteration: it is concrete in view of its isolated form, but also concrete in view of what happened that night and its *tremendum*.

If I speak about the topography of Mauthausen, I cannot omit these documentary elements. In the linguistic heritage of National Socialism, there are not only Hans Baumann's Hitler Youth songs—we sang them on our marches, at flag consecrations, and at morning ceremonies: their style, full of ideals, soon turned into a murderous landscape determined by political calculation, which felt itself bound to ostensibly rational goals that were in truth unfathomable. The linguistic legacy bears witness to this.

The alphabet of German fascism is composed of words of death. But these words of death speak not of death, rather of BEING EMIGRATED / of PROCESSING / of PACIFICATION CAMPAIGNS / of PURIFICATION / of DISINFECTION / of DISINFESTATION / of TOTAL YIELDS / of LARGE MOBILIZATIONS / of PREPARING THE JEWS / of J-CAMPAIGNS / of J-TRANSPORTS / of the TRANSFER OF CHILDREN / of RESTORING THE PEACE / of SPECIAL TRAIN TRAFFIC / of SPECIAL ACCOMMODATIONS / of ST or SPECIAL TREATMENT / of GV or GASSING VEHICLES, and have to do with the fact that the act of LOADING CARGO leads to the doors of the gas truck.

(1996)

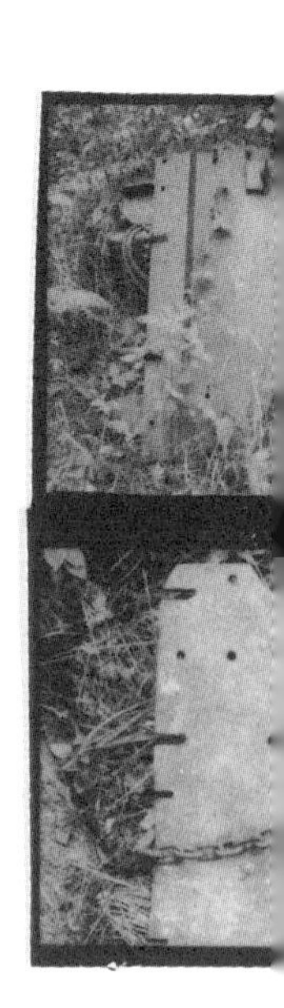

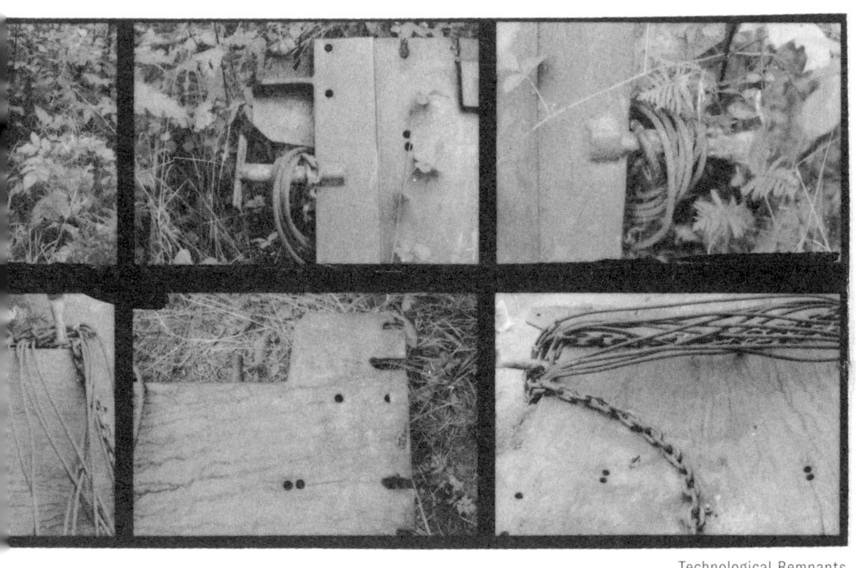

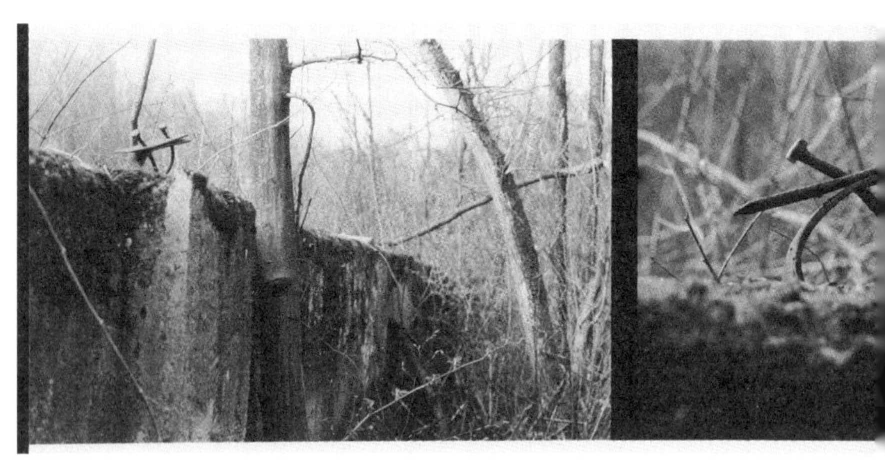

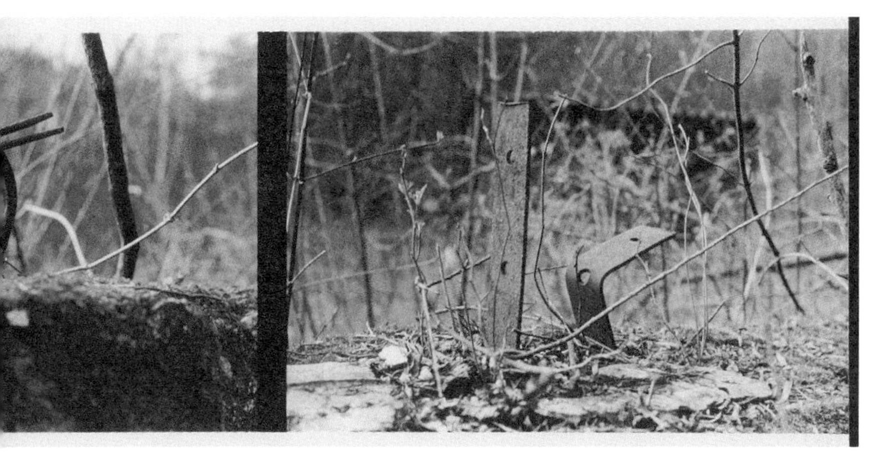

Iron Remnants in the Foundation of the Great Hall of the Mauthausen Concentration Camp

In the name and subject index to *Mein Kampf*, the entries for "Judaism" add up to 39 lines. No entry is longer, except for "National Socialism."

From one vagueness to the next—this permanently acute situation gives the usurper the opportunity to act "resolutely." He is the beneficiary of fragmentariness, burrowing his way into the permanently open wound.

H. reproduced his father's extreme authority and invented a family for himself in which he could set the tone, along with a pliable concept: *Volksgemeinschaft*, racial community (which included the hoodlum and the Prussian Premier). The most important thing is the One Man who towers over all the others (and, with these dimensions, does not actually belong to them). In a grammatically questionable turn of phrase, he claims: I am all of you, *ich bin Ihr*. In this cracked logic lie his success with imbecilic believers and his failure with the English, who did not let themselves get mixed up in what this provincial man from the Innviertel intended with his concept.

Hollow idealism—glued together by a sense of providence (not tied to anything specific), myth instead of *ratio*—turned into mean vulgarity and was stamped with the swastika, passed on in elite training schools, and set in front of a youth incapable of differentiating.

The man of the mob has the force of the mob, not just his own force. If he were only a single man and a single force…—but he has the force of the mob.

Mein Kampf: a head beats against mirages full of content suggested to it. (To have written this forty years ago! Today, it's not dangerous.)

The individual as order, as idea, as delusion
In the name of an order, an idea, a delusion
Resistance to ideality (order, ideals, delusion) is the weakest resistance of all.
One quickly becomes willing, all that's needed is an appeal to the delusional self.
On a lower level: obedience, racial community;
on a middle level: ideal-filled reflection, a play of façades;
on a higher level: aura, grace, stigmatization (and delusional adoration of the stigmatized).

H. He had no taste. He had his private morality, but he had no taste. A merely aesthetic differentiation? A lack of taste opens one up to incitation and moralizing, making do with two concepts when considering heterogeneity, savoring banality as truth and adopting as truth the card that trumps. His "morality" is not affected, it cannot be in its gelatinous state.

"A *Volk* on a quest, driven by divine will" (Heimrad B., 1943)—the *Volk*, the race or people, the divine: unverifiably universal, it overflows into the ideal, which is projection and introjection at the same time, secretion and inhalation, something that is sufficient unto itself (onanism of the Third Reich).

Hitler's identification with the power of the father. Projection of this power onto his audience, who feel themselves (via secondary identification) to be one with Hitler's power and insinuated love.

"Ideals" as substitutes for thinking, distractions from concrete and careful differentiation. Exaggeration, swelling, monstrosity. Since ideals replace truth without being bound to truth's limits, since their irrational coloration makes them invulnerable, opposition means heresy, with all the consequences.

The most commonly used instrument for punishment was their fathers' hand. However, many fathers also used belts, sticks, and whips (72%). Four Green Berets stated that their fathers resorted to using "any object they could get their hands on," and two of them reported that their fathers also occasionally used boards, iron rods, or chains.

"There where our deficiencies lie we revel in rapturous enthusiasm" (Nietzsche, *Dawn*, aphorism 377). For H., was being the strong man lack and fantasy? His youth could lead one to that conclusion. Hitler as suppressed, the one barely fit for life? Then his hubris, derived from being weakened, squalid (selling watercolors door to door)? He stayed the same, collecting money and votes door to door. And German politics quickly reduced itself to selling dubious goods at fantastic prices.

Parody: Röhm, even after being shot, "My Führer! My Führer!"

No matter how hypothetical the stimulus, H. reacted to the point of exhaustion with his complete neural and verbal inventory.

Göring: political liqueur.

H.: a resigned type, whose resignation overflows to hide his intimacy with death. The Germans' love was for a defeated man (politically, this was extremely dangerous), which is why the tie to him was so strong, the belief in him without any kind of criteria that could have kept it in check. Women were quick to sense the sentimentality of his main trait, suffering. If sentimentality turns into action and saving oneself gets confused with saving everyone else, then those who doubt the suggested salvation—bound like a twin to destruction—are lost.

Even a gathering of hats as an audience would have satisfied his affects.

The radical right H. as a type: the worker without fatherland. His self-mythologization kept him from having and respecting a fatherland. For politicians, fatherland has to

be a value (for reflective thinking, it may well remain il-
lusory); his inflated self, however, knew only his bloated
Reich and a number of the population he could count on.
In his moments of sentimental fatherlandiness, he missed
the mark even more fundamentally. Fatherland—a concept that alienated his self (and in this he was not unlike
an artist, except that artists have nothing to do with secret
services and armies, with nonprivate means).

H.—a clot.

First, he put an end to the Weimar Republic, then to Weimar, which has been known as Buchenwald ever since.

"The great wars of the present are the effects of the study
of history" (Nietzsche, *Dawn*, aphorism 180). If that is the
case, then the orientation and aim of that study—Times
of Greatness—should be changed, in a process of neutral-
ization and disenchantment, starting in kindergarten and
elementary school.

A propaganda man steps down. There lie the corpses of his
children and wife, victims of his fateful gift for historical

stage effects. Death of an intellectual (which is what he is constantly called)? An intellectual, what's that? Not Goebbels.

Functioning democracy. Military leaders submit themselves to their soldiers' judgment. Strong impression of this in Xenophon. Even in the direst straits, no authoritarian decisions.

A saint's face and a saint's life, a deception designed by his spookmaster Goebbels. Mind and seduction of the mind are provided for. How many thousands were full of "ideals" (that always suffices) and surrendered themselves for a phantom, for the public enemy number one, the actual conspirator in the simple soldier's uniform, master of demagogy and the rhino whip, the "skunk" (Salomo Friedlaender), the "rabid dog" (Tresckow, Stauffenberg), the "incarnation of evil" (Yorck before Judge Freisler). He is still ruining lives. Some are gone and some will not be rid of him until their death, cannot shake him, his and their existences demand incessant rectification.

firms are not required to provide reports about causes of death and related matters, that made work easier for the manager, the recording clerk, and the typist. before, they always had to get their heads together to decide on an appropriate formulation, but now there was no need to get their heads together or agonize about it. If someone collapsed, it was his own thing, no one asked him anything before and no one asked anything afterward, they let him lie there for a while, and then it was over.

Treitschke: "Without heroes and hero worship, a people will perish." A people that perishes from heroes and hero worship thirsts for heroes and hero worship, and so on.

When he was able (because others had made it possible) to carry out a function that had to do with a great deal of blood, silence, and lamentation, the blood and lamentation of many people, that is when it was over for his brain's rudimentary capacity to grasp a thought. It cannot be said that he couldn't come to grips with the situation, since that would have required an ability to grasp things. It wasn't that he couldn't come to grips with the situation, because he couldn't grasp anything, and there was also not anything to grasp, other than these three sentences about terror: "I cannot deny my share of personal guilt in all this. But it is in a ratio of 1 to 70 million. The ratio is small; still, it is there" (*Last Letters from Stalingrad*).

Melancholy: The shadow of the object fell upon the ego (Freud).

The will to forget, and the will not to forget—that's not what counts. Horror disregards these differentiations.

Democracy that is kept in check and that keeps in check excludes murder as a pragmatic or fantasy method for education and purification. Since fascism grew out of opposition to democracy, it moved quickly from cudgels in the first hours to crematoria in the last.

Mein Kampf: "In four days, our regiment had shrunk from 3 ½ thousand men to 600. We were left with only 3 officers. 4 companies had to be dissolved. But we were all proud of having beaten the English," and so forth until the last days of April 1945, paraphrase of Heine's "Hymn": "Round about me lie the corpses of my friends, but we have conquered." Inscription: From this place, on August 4, 1914, the Eighth Infantry Battalion went to battle. 36 officers and 1222 soldiers. 36 officers and 1221 men fell in battle.

"weighed down by corpses" (Marcus Aurelius).

(1987)

CONCRETE POETRY

1

what good can a word be once it is "used," once it lies around only in order to be fit into a speech, to be an object, a seat for something. what does a word sound like that has gone through kindergarten, high school, and acting lessons?

2

it would be arbitrary and an all-too-convenient solution to ignore the historicity of language in favor of closed formations (the dictionary, for example; culture, for example). society forces us to accept that its continued existence requires that it stand firm. we are not able to force it to accept this: we are lost if we stand firm. so we provide that firmness with movement, differentiation, utopia (but not a flag), we provide starting points, critique, analyses (of, for example, how someone who writes remains alive by changing the artistic means of expression).

3

more than anything, bob cobbing would like to spray printer's ink through a screen to be free of society's most cumbersome relict: preformed speech, which reduces language to formulae that appear en masse. repeating these formulae and estranging them through repetition is the first step of concrete speech; the second, reflecting and breaking open the brutality of the familiar; the third, formulating material in a new way.

4

concretization of the nonconcrete. materialization of the immaterial.

5

josef bauer spills letters out in front of you: that's every-thing for you, that's what you are: incapable of articulation. but start anyway: concretize your existence: create a basis for yourself: build a constellation!

6

new poetry writes a new language. it separates itself from the usual gibberish, which has nothing to offer except ci-tations, irony's material for analysis. new poetry writes not in or by means of new language: instead, as poetry is being written, the capacity for speech and for having language realizes itself in a new, fresh way.

7

destructive forces are at work where a form found and de-veloped in a certain historical-linguistic situation has been passed on for so long that it is worn out and no longer ef-fective. in the moment of writing, every author must create for themselves the formal foundation of their poetry if they do not want to get ensnared in convention. they must free themselves, even from the conventions of the new poetry, from the available formulae found by poets from august stramm to franz mon.

8

concrete writing excludes or isolates contexts related to

content. and do contexts even really exist, in so-called reality? is context not perforated by the non-contextual? content remains only as relicts, data, impressions. continuity is achieved not in reality, but in linguistic presentation. the disproportionate and semantically fragile is made linguistically proportionate, semantically precise. overcoming vagueness through form.

9

contents (pieces of evidence for external reality) are reduced to linguistic data. syntax is given leave to vacation in the south or for the virtue and hygiene of the white race: syntax is taken apart to show the ostensible contexts that it actually represents.

10

ever since eugen gomringer's and friedrich achleitner's CONSTELLATIONS, the expansion of artistic means includes the visual formation of a text. writing's kineticism does not settle down in straight lines, in closed sentences or pages. it follows motor stimuli, optical needs, and sensual impulses. individual words or individual letters become signs that are no longer only semantic, but function as compact, encoded units of information that can be decoded.

11

the surface becomes a space of evocation. the space calls forth words, and words determine the space. in this kind of literature, there is no longer any writing paper, no pages that are just used. pages as materialized surfaces are a moment in the realization of a text, like the canvas in painting.

whatever is text is simultaneously a spatial element; linguistic realization is simultaneously optical realization; and semantic information is simultaneously aesthetic information. something is not written beautifully, but is text as writing. if one sticks to this differentiation, one will no longer misunderstand the new poetry—or this form of new poetry. in a fritz lichtenauer text-image, something is not illustrated graphically, something said is not enriched after the fact with an aesthetic dimension; instead, text and image are one. aesthetic information does not provide additional information about a piece of semantic information; that is, an aggregate of meaning is not aestheticized after the fact, but rather: something unified is sought and displayed.

(1973)

ON THE ARPEIRON:
RESPONSE TO A SURVEY ABOUT THE AVANT-GARDE TODAY

The Viennese journal Profile *asked a group of Austrian writers if the term "avant-garde" means or ever meant anything for their writing.*

1. The concept "avant-garde" has dissipated for me ever since there have been complete editions and selected works and since the permanent production of new methods has become the standard *habitus* ("everything is possible"). When anything is possible at any moment, this deprives the concept of its substance; in other words: there is no longer an "avant-garde," because the battle is over. Our actions now take place on a pacified field.

2. When someone who writes poetry is at their wits' end and, like me (everyone works on their own legend), cannot advance a single step and does not want to move a single step backward into the former state of things; when destructive, dated sonnet-scribbling has had its time, then, one morning between Hallein and Salzburg (in a "Center for Adult Education"), there comes along this passage by Helmut Heissenbüttel (*Topographien*, 1954):

> from deep but from : since : since-color since-taste
> since-feeling : word this : since word : unallowed
> unmowed word-figure possibility shoulderflesh
> lipflesh wordlipflesh : deep from : since from

invisibly since : to say substituteworddeepwithin :
to talk to speak to chat to prattle : ever in each ever
at each time : since this : deadline having passed
deadline having been eaten up in : not not in : since
notallowed notspok'n not advised : topic not topic
from deeply untopic from deeply from : since

That was it for an attitude full of ideals, I turned away from
my overtaxed individuality and toward the phenomena of
language.

3. "a bunch of rotten and decaying words are coming along
the rue de maine" (Hansjörg Zauner, *Jolly*, 1999). That was
what it was about, saving oneself from word rot (the mel-
ancholic line—"And o'er the mountains hung the night,"
from Goethe's 1775 "Welcome and Farewell"—is not what
is meant here).

4. Worn-down speech, speech that can be used for anything, speech that does not intend what is said (the slogan),
the speech that forms bubbles that are understood without
understanding, the speech gushing out of the non-person,
soaking and flooding everything. Then: concretion, becom-
ing aware, and the forming of a new word out of what one
has become aware of—

5. New poetry separates itself from the usual gibberish,
which has nothing to offer except citations, irony's material
for analysis. New poetry writes not in or by means of new
language: instead, as poetry is being written, the capacity

for speech and for having language realizes itself in a new, fresh way. (Heimrad Bäcker, "concrete poetry," 1973)

6. The insistent, intransigent work with language, "desirous of a new, strange stimulus form" (Franz Mon), not letting up, throwing all form-energy and life-energy into one undertaking: the avant-garde of Büchner, who included long passages from French Revolution trial proceedings in his *Danton*, using the thing-like nature of the proceedings for his own purpose: anticipation of the practice of montage. How is what Achleitner did in "preparations for an execution" any different? (*transcript*, too, took this path.)

7. The wealth of inventions that we attribute to the avant-garde (for reasons we can more or less justify) pits itself against a century of uninhibited word consumption. The wealth of inventions, the new ways of speaking, but the many *Führer* efface them all. The *Führer* do not tolerate articulation. They ladle out word-consuming mush. Schwitters and Hausmann in exile, Serner deported "to the East," Carl Einstein's suicide. Does it not speak for both avant-gardes (in 1920 and 1950) that they arose in the wake of wars and great crimes (committed with an instrumentarium of ideals on a bureaucratic base)?

8. The letting-up of the avant-garde's intensity gives preformed speech the opportunity to submerge the world in the same sloganeering mediocrity that the avant-garde pulled the world out of. The letting-up of intensity appears in the lack of formal inventions. But what happens when Arp writes this poem:

Is it true

that the arp

seeks

the arpeiron

There are moments of deep agreement with the body of language as it has been passed down, agreement with poetic speech that has been liberated from sloganeering and that has nothing simplistic about it.

Arp is the master of this language. Did he not publish *Der Vogel selbdritt* already in 1920?

9. Kulka, Stramm, Hugo Ball, Schwitters—just a few names from among the most superb explorations of what the literature of this century can be. In literary history after 1910, there is a pronounced inclination for the linguistically unusual. A principle comes to be applied that was identified as one of internal linguistic change and free syntax. Heissenbüttel, *Second Frankfurt Lecture*, 1963: "In the history of this literary transformation of language, there are the examples of twentieth-century literature that remain the most contentious even today. From Velimir Khlebnikov to François Dufrêne and Franz Mon, from the Italian Futurists' *parole in libertà* and Guillaume Apollinaire's *Calligrammes* to the visual and concrete poetry of the present and to attempts to typographize even very long texts, from Joyce's *Finnegans Wake* to Michel Butor's *Mobile*, from Carl Einstein's *Bebuquin* to Hans G. Helms…" And of course Schwitters. He makes a millennium out of the century.

K.S.

with the rake
of a stingray
schwitt scythes
blooms
schwittering bitter
ness and crumbs

10. The avant-garde cannot define itself without giving up its claim to be something like what it is. I make a text. If it is successful, it can be attributed to the Carolingian Renaissance or this century's avant-garde; if it is just mediocre, then it doesn't matter if it operates under one brand name or another.

Avant-garde is not a concept (of course, it is that, in addition to other things), but a state. If the concept is silently withdrawn, nothing changes for literature. The transformation of artistic means of expression can hardly be influenced by a concept (which is not subject to the same dynamism as literature). And yet we operate with this concept. It is "practicable." But it does not help to open up the arpeiron.

(2000)

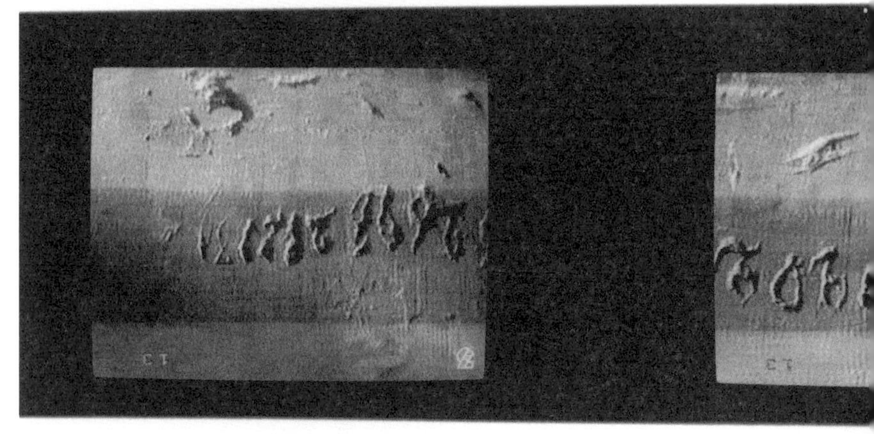

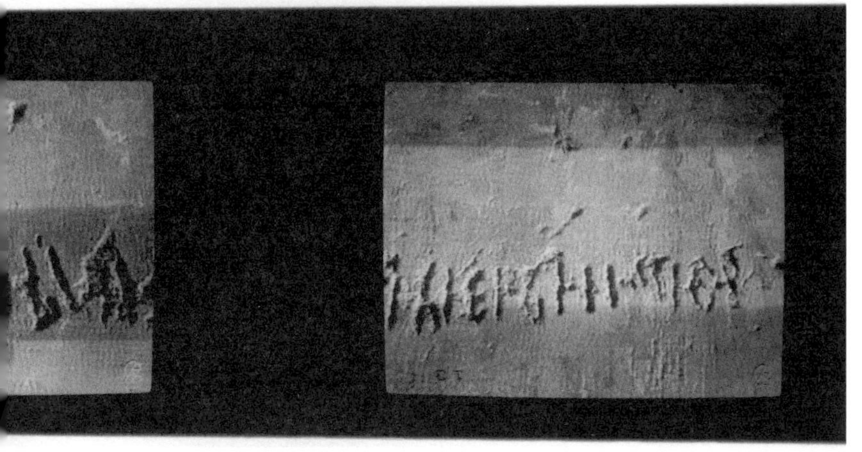

Photographs from Television: Gestapo Cellar in Cologne

THE TRUTH OF KILLING: AN INTERVIEW BY JUDITH VEICHTLBAUER AND STEPHAN STEINER

In your author's bios, unlike most people of your generation, you've never concealed your adolescent enthusiasm for National Socialism.

I joined the Party when I was eighteen and started working as part of the regional leadership of the Hitler Youth. During that period, I wrote articles about things like shooting contests and regional sport meets. The method developed by Baldur von Schirach, the head of the Hitler Youth, consisted of an incremental ensnarement of young people: hiking quickly turned into field exercises, and then came shooting. This gave me, who was disabled by polio as a child, the opportunity to be included in a community. No one ever brought up my disability, despite Nazi ideology. "Being part of something" is a category that has to be considered for young people who don't yet have the ability to differentiate, an ability that requires knowledge gained from good teachers, perhaps, or from work in a union or a party. Without that, you were at the mercy of the Third Reich's idealistic façade.

Other than this experience of community, were there tangible changes in your daily life that made the 1938 annexation of Austria by Nazi Germany, the Anschluss, seem like a push toward modernization at first?

Yes, my parents, who were both unemployed, were able to move out of their basement apartment and into an apartment with a bathroom for the first time. In the First Republic, there was no civil marriage, so my mother, who was divorced, couldn't marry my stepfather until after the Anschluss, despite the fact that they already had three kids! This feeling of an economic boom was very short-lived, though, and as a child you aren't aware of the downside. On top of that, this thirteen-year-old was impressed by so many people's enthusiastic "yes" for Hitler.

You weren't aware of the other side of these developments—the total grip on society and the existence of concentration camps?

About the concentration camps, everyone always said, "That's where the worst criminals are!" Although we were just a few kilometers from Mauthausen, we didn't know what really happened there. As a member of the Hitler Youth, I myself never witnessed or participated in any act of violence. I could have just been lucky. However, I must say, the final two years were risky for me, because the authoritarian habitus had taken shape in me too. Even if didn't commit atrocities, I would have become someone who acted in an authoritarian way. I use Freud's expression "psychic infection" for this, because it really is a type of infection.

How did you free yourself from these formative experiences?

At the end of the war, I was taken to Mauthausen by the Americans and saw what took place there. I didn't understand the full extent of it. Only through continuous reflection and by noticing the long-lasting susceptibility to Nazi ideology's ideal-filled nonsense did I gradually distance myself from that way of thinking. In 1945, as someone who hadn't been persecuted, the idea that we had been liberated, as opposed to conquered, didn't mean anything to me. The fact that a cousin of mine disappeared in Hartheim, a killing center for people with mental and physical disabilities, is something that I only became aware of later. The feeling of liberation only set in much later. And now, I have to say, I get aggressive when someone denies that the end of the war was in fact a liberation.

What role did your engagement with existential philosophy play in this learning process?

The categories of existential philosophy marked a significant break in my thinking. At first, I was planning to write a dissertation about Dostoyevsky, but then I decided on Karl Jaspers. My question back then about the relation of the individual and society—in which Heidegger's thinking about humanity's temporality and historicity were also important—still occupies me today. I also agree with Sartre's insistence on communication among human beings as an expression of dependency on the Other, especially because the century's most terrible murderers annulled it. But Sartre's turn to Marxism was something I couldn't relate to—I recoiled from it as yet another absolutist aspiration. I never made it to the point of being a Marxist, so to speak, but I do believe, like Robert Musil, that socialism is a necessity.

The preoccupation with the phenomenon of National Socialism and especially with its politics of annihilation hasn't let go of you. For a quarter century, you've been working on your transcript *project, which has accompanied your process of reflection. How is it distinguished from common literary methods?*

For me, as it was for Hermann Broch, literature is a learning process that I am at the center of, as someone who was living back then and is still alive. *transcript*'s method is not narrative. I restrict myself completely to documents, which include bureaucratic records, orders, meeting minutes, but also the accounts of those who experienced the camps. Working with them has been my daily occupation for decades, and I accumulate a great deal of information, without using a computer. It isn't just my "topic," it's my life's work.

In the Vienna Group's new literary approaches, and Helmut Heissenbüttel's, I found a way to take this material up into literature. Unfortunately, concrete literature has failed to take on this inventory of documents, which in itself creates concrete forms that only have to be transferred over. In my texts, there's a materiality, a clear conceptual aspect, and my inspiration or imagination doesn't matter, nothing is narratively expanded on. I aim for the place where the document becomes identical with the text, and when it's possible, I adopt the document exactly as it is. I think narrative forms are mostly incapable of adequately comprehending what happened, while the methods of *transcript* can grasp its monumental terror.

How do people react to this radical attitude toward writing? Was there the reproach that it was too formalistic?

Hermann Langbein wrote in a letter that my work had "a compelling force." With *transcript*, I was surprised to learn that, after some initial difficulties, even people who didn't really know what to do with modern literature had a very precise understanding of my intention as an artist. The elements of my writing are extreme and not susceptible to misinterpretation. My starting point is the defeated individual facing the collective's distorted grimace. I make audible the voice of the individual subjected to overwhelming forces. The statements that I emphasize may contain a kind of conservatism. It's a conventional language, it's how people speak with one another, it has yet to be so destroyed that I can't cite it. In a statement like "you will find my body before you get to the school. you can come pick me up right away," the speaker's own end is reflected upon, and in the moment of writing this, its author has moved outside of time, even if this is not actually possible. Time ruins them, but they are still able to say, you can come pick me up right away, that is, me, the one who will be lying there.

And I look for statements like this, in which someone in charge of an experiment notes: "after breathing ceased, i had the experimental subject wagner brought back to life by increasing the pressure." This statement reveals the cold, violent mindset of the person subjecting another individual to a planned process. Here, "having someone brought back to life" is shorthand for a monstruous act. When I come upon a sentence like this, I know it belongs in the book.

For your texts, text-based works, and photographs, you often use the term "epitaph." Can you explain that term?

As an example, I have a page on which there are only Polish first names, and if one knows that Poles attach a stronger meaning to first names than to family names, then a series like this, of first names of people who were killed, is an epitaph for me. It's a narrow band that extends from the top of the page to the bottom. I don't have to add anything, and it has an effect all by itself. That's the connection to the *tremendum* that I give to the concrete, a connection to horror that the human being living unhistorically would very much like to disregard. In these epitaphs, the truth of killing breaks through. This paradoxical conceptual pair— truth and killing—became reality in Auschwitz.

Can the term "aesthetics" even be used in connection with your texts? Or to put it another way: how can one stop the written documentation of terror in the context of transcript from being transformed into something that is "aesthetically beautiful"?

The so-called "aesthetic," which can also be a quality in a good sense, is reduced by me to a linguistic nakedness in which there are barely any literary elements present in the way that one generally likes them. It is a reduction and selection among all the possible aesthetic formations that determines whether something belongs in my *transcript* project. There's always the risk of slipping into the aesthetic and crossing over a very fine line. There's a real danger if you don't work through this, there's a real danger if you let up on the intensity of that line!

Do you see a problem, like Ruth Klüger does, when memory is musealized?

It would not seem right to me if Auschwitz were allowed to fall into disrepair and were planted over. It's part of our history. The camps should be maintained, but maybe in a less polished form than in Mauthausen, where everything was freshly painted and the camp's main avenue asphalted just in time for the Pope's visit in 1988.

Your photographic work also focuses in this sense on a documentation of relicts, the material traces of what happened...

Yes, and to name an example, I tried to photograph the remaining walls in Mauthausen in their fearsome thingness, so that their violence would become visible. I was there a few hundred times, and I kept trying to do this over and over again. I also documented Mauthausen's subcamps: for example, in Gusen, the building where the day's orders were given existed until recently, when it was renovated as a residential villa. It was incomprehensible to me that it was not included in the Mauthausen Memorial. The main avenue in the Gusen camp was built up with single-family houses after the war, but the former camp brothel was still recognizable for decades, with its windowpanes that were painted over to keep people from looking in. To systematize all the material I've collected, I would probably need two years. I would like to include them in a volume of documentation along with a concentrated selection of the most recent literature. The materials would be backed up with historical references.

And your work has also been realized as concrete objects...

Yes. For example, I designed a memorial in Engerwitzdorf for resistance fighters from the town of Freistadt who were executed by order of the Nazi Gauleiter Eigruber when the post-Nazi Renner government was already in office in Vienna. My memorial plaques are there, with the names of the victims and the word "executed" as a concrete series that continues from metal plate to metal plate.

Your work on your transcript *project has absorbed all your writerly ambitions. Does that signify a loss for you?*

Gitta Sereny speaks of a spiritual and moral death that was inflicted back then on almost everyone alive as a thinking and feeling being. That knowledge has determined my entire existence. I'm lucky to be able to continue pursuing this process as a seventy-year-old. It is also a kind of victory for me to read someone like Zygmunt Bauman, to whom we owe a paradigm shift in sociology, who no longer considers National Socialism a mere accident in history, but instead shows how society produces authoritarian characters and elements. The need to write poems and texts that do not have a connection to *transcript* is completely gone, I can no longer do that, and I'm not sorry about it. Even though I put together a collection of good poems that was published by the Rainer Verlag, I would never have become an author on the level of a Reinhard Priessnitz. So it's better to just let it be.

(1995/2011)

SEASCAPE

transcription

B. 36 War log, size: A3

Location, wind, weather,

sea state, lighting conditions,

visibility, moonlight, etc.

Incidents[3])

0430   Qu. AL 0196, SW 5,

dry, rough seas, good

visibility, overcast.

0800   Qu. AL 0175, SW 4/5,

         heavy rain, moderate seas,

         poor visibility.

1215   Qu. AL 1973, SW 4/5,

heavy rain, rising sea,

moderate rough swell, clear.

Sighted lifeboat of the Norwegian motor tanker *John P. Pederson* drifting under sail. Three survivors were lying exhausted under a tarpaulin and only showed themselves as the boat was moving away again. They stated that their ship had been torpedoed 28 days before. I turned down their request to be taken aboard, provisioned the boat with food and water, and gave them the course and distance to the Icelandic coast. Boat and crew were in a state that, in view of the prevailing weather, offered hardly any prospects of rescue.

1600   AK 0357, SSE 4, dry,

moderate seas, high

southerly swell, hazy.

2000   Qu. AK 3956, ESE 6,

rain, very rough seas, poor

visibility, overcast.

2400   Qu. AK 0261, strong

gusts of wind from the north

5-6, heavy rain, very rough

seas, poor visibility, overcast.

0400   Qu. AK 2930, NW 5–

6, dry, very rough seas,

poor visibility, overcast.

Headings and information pr on foot of second page /
hw slash under addressee list / title p ur (through and
below "incidents"): "Wr 111777" (hw) / r below "U
71" check mark / ll: "enc. 55 of" (hw), stamped "1. Sea
command 17822/41 top secret" (hw "/41" inserted)

Reference: IMT (International Military Tribunal: Nuremberg, 1949), Vol. XIV, 340–1; Vol. XXXV, 623–5.

TRANSCRIPT Z

dry Oswiecim kcher sy baro
in Auschwitz, there is a big house

1.

Professor von Verschuer to Professor Fischer, 20 May 37
Professor von Verschuer to Professor Fischer, 5
November 37
Professor Fischer to Professor von Verschuer, 10
December 38: "Your proposal for the study of the Gypsy
question is very good."

2.

The distinction between those to be eliminated and
those worthy of advancement in our society is of
the utmost importance if we wish to safeguard our
hereditary endowment and our race. It is desirable that
such registers be set up throughout the Reich so that we
may combat the asocial mentality with all the means at
our disposal.

3.

The sex life and love life of the blond and the dark
I. Anthropological section,
The sex life and love life of the blond and the dark
II. Cultural history section.

4.

Many men among the gypsies were in the World War and
fought for the Fatherland as much as any others but that
has been ignored by Dr. Portschy. He Speaks and Writes
not to give the gypsies anything, not to allow them any

work or other entitlements so I have just decided to call
on the High Government. the police has been called on
us in a way that one should not be treated in speeches
and in words the way it has been declared one is often
treated roughly as if the Führer did not care for us and
as if we were hostile to the Party or endangered it. since
we are Roman Catholic of Aryan descent and have always
been so I see myself forced to raise a complaint for all of
us with the High Reich Government.

5.
Z

ZM+

ZM

ZM−

NZ

6.
As before, countless official enquiries, affecting the
safeguarding of our hereditary endowment, were
answered by the Gypsy Archives of our research section.

7.
The youngest inmate in the Camp Register was recorded
as Stefan Czernikiewicz, Number 7785, a two-month-old
Polish gypsy.
The youngest inmate in the Camp Register (Women)
was recorded as Viktoria Dittlof, Number 8502, a one-
month-old Polish gypsy.

8.

The number of racially resolved cases is currently 21,498. After completion of the securing operation, over 9,000 mixed-race gypsies were able to be concentrated by the police in a special gypsy camp.

9.

The number Z-8232 is given to Josef Horwath, who is born on June 6, 1943, in the Gypsy Camp in Birkenau. He dies on June 26, 1943.

The number Z-8233 is given to Johann Horwath, who is born on June 4, 1943, in the Gypsy Camp in Birkenau; he dies on June 26, 1943.

The number Z-8234 is given to a boy born on June 2, 1943, in the Gypsy Camp in Birkenau; he dies on June 9, 1943.

The number Z-8235 is given to Franz Daniel, who is born on June 1, 1943, in the Birkenau Gypsy Camp, he dies on June 9, 1943.

10.

The gypsies called Doctor Mengele "daddy." The women went to him, fell on their knees in front of him, kissed his hand, and kept saying to him, "Daddy, when can we leave here?"

11.

Mengele infected identical and fraternal Jewish and gypsy twins with the same quantity of typhoid bacteria, took blood at various times for chemical analysis in Berlin, and followed the course of the disease. The epidemics "raging" in Auschwitz,

12.

An entire family of eight was killed in this way so that their heterochromatic eyes could be sent to the Dahlem Institute.

13.

In addition to the usual problems—lack of space, catastrophic sanitary conditions, rising rates of illness, excessive mortality—it was the gypsy children, who were suffering from the children's disease noma and, despite the cancer-like tumors and stinking gangrene, still smiled from deep within their feverish eyes, who got to Pohl. The bright gaze of those little disheveled creatures, standing motionless under the deep blue sky in front of the greenish horse-stall barracks, with the two massive smokestacks on the left-hand side, and to the right, a thick white cloud of smoke coming from the forest—in front of this image, Pohl must have realized that his administration had broken all the laws of ethics and would be forever marked.

14.

But the Commander said, "Oh, they're just Gypsies."

15.

Of the total of 20,943 Gypsies registered as prisoners
in Auschwitz, 3,461 were transferred to other camps.
The rest died by starvation, disease, or gas. After 2,897
children, women, and men (including former soldiers
of the Wehrmacht) were driven into the gas chambers
on the night of August 2–3, 1944, there were no more
Gypsies left in Auschwitz.

16.

3 double-muffle cremation ovens
5 three-muffle cremation ovens
5 three-muffle cremation ovens
1 eight-muffle cremation oven
1 eight-muffle cremation oven

17.

Fear of more blows, the ghastly sight of piled-up corpses,
the biting smoke, the humming of fans and the flickering
of flames, the whole infernal chaos had paralyzed my
sense of orientation as well as my ability to think. I was
like one hypnotized and obeyed each order.

18.

I'm happy I wasn't there by the Third Reich and
everything that was there ... Lots of people were killed,
in camps they were exterminated, people wanted to
exterminate them, the whole Sinti. I don't look back
at that so much, but I still believe that a shadow is on
the gadje still, a shadow, really, I've heard that so many
times, lots of people have said that, that if Hitler were

still around, then all you would have been gassed a long
time ago, and things like that, right? I think, young
people aren't like that anymore, they're not like that at
all, but there are still people that say that and that casts a
big shadow on the gadje.

i'm not able to answer that
i don't have any answer
i don't remember
i did not explain that
i have to say i can't remember
i can't remember anymore
no
i had nothing to do with prisoners
i have only a dim recollection
numbers this large were not, to my knowledge,
no that is not my signature
i can't cite individual cases anymore
i don't remember
i never stood at the entrance
that testimony does not correspond to the truth
no i was not on the ramp
i don't remember any transport
i don't know who was in charge of commercial
operations
i don't remember
i couldn't say any longer
i couldn't say what kinds of measures were taken
i never performed any kind of duty on the ramp
i don't know anything about any sonderkommando
i issued no order and i also don't believe

but i can't remember
i don't remember either
i was never part of any consultation
i don't remember either
i never stated that i
i can't really positively remember it
i was never aware of that
i never had any experience like that
i'm not familiar with that concept
i can't remember

NOTES:

1: Professor Otmar von Verschuer, Institute Head, Kaiser Wilhelm Institute of Anthropology, Berlin-Dahlem; Professor Eugen Fischer, Director of the Kaiser-Wilhelm Institute: founding figures in the anthropological research on Sinti and Roma.

4: Letter from Franz Horvath from Redlschlag (Region of Unterwarth, Austria), May 12, 1938; Dr. Tobias Portschy, Nazi-era governor of the State of Burgenland.

5: Abbreviations for "Gypsy" (Z), "Mixed-race Gypsy" (ZM), and "Non-Gypsy" (NZ).

10: Dr. Josef Mengele, assistant to Professor von Verschuer and Camp Doctor in Auschwitz.

13: Oswald Pohl, Director of the SS Main Economic and Administrative Office and Head of the Concentration Camps.

18: Gerhard F. Rüdiger, conversation with Meggi Patay-Reinhardt.

BIBLIOGRAPHY:

Danuta Czech, *Auschwitz Chronicle*

Wilfried Daim, *Der Mann, der Hitler die Ideen gab* [The man who gave Hitler his ideas]

Documentation Archive of the Austrian Resistance, *Widerstand und Verfolgung in Burgenland, 1934–1945* [Resistance and persecution in Burgenland, 1934–1945]

Gideon Greif, *We Wept Without Tears: Testimonies of the Jewish Sonderkommando from Auschwitz*

Hermann Langbein, *Der Auschwitz Prozeß* [The Auschwitz trial]

Benno Müller-Hill, *Murderous Science: Elimination by Scientific Selection of Jews, Gypsies, and Others, Germany 1933–1945*

Jean-Claude Pressac, *Auschwitz: Technique and Operation of the Gas Chambers*

Tilman Zülch, *In Auschwitz vergast, bis heute verfolgt* [Gassed in Auschwitz, still persecuted today]

NOTES ON TEXTS AND IMAGES

NOTES ON THE TEXTS

All texts appear courtesy of Thomas Eder, and all photos appear courtesy of Michael Merighi and the Museum of Modern Art, Vienna. All translations in this edition are by Patrick Greaney, except for the first essay in the collection, which was translated by Patrick Greaney and Jacquelyn Pied.

<u>DOCUMENTARY POETRY:</u> originally published as "Dokumentarische Dichtung" in *Protokolle*, 29.2 (1992), 43–5. An earlier version of this English translation was first published as the chapbook *Documentary Poetry,* trans. Jacquelyn Pied and Patrick Greaney (Calgary: No Press, 2014).

Heinrich Himmler was the head of the SS (abbreviation for *Schutzstaffel*, Protective Squad), which planned and implemented the Shoah. In a 1943 speech to SS members, he described how they *remained decent* while carrying out mass killings, acts that would later be recognized, he claimed, as part of a *glorious chapter in German history.*

The *Wannsee Conference* was a meeting of Nazi leaders in January 1942 in a villa on the outskirts of Berlin. Participants included Reinhard Heydrich, Himmler's deputy, and Adolf Eichmann, who oversaw the logistics of the Shoah. They discussed the plan to murder all European Jews. Bäcker frequently quotes notes from the meeting—in this and other essays, as well as in *transcript*—as key examples of the language of the Shoah.

Operation Reinhard was a 1941 plan to kill all the Jews in German-occupied Poland. It was coordinated by *Odilo Globocnik* and included the establishment of the *Belzec, Sobibor,* and *Treblinka* killing centers, in which about 1.5 million Jews were killed.

MIRRORING: originally published as "Widerspiegelung," in *Die Rampe* 3 (1994), 59–63.

Being emigrated … : here, Bäcker lists euphemisms and obfuscatory phrases from Nazi documents.

ON THE TOPOGRAPHY OF MAUTHAUSEN: originally published as "Mauthausen: Beiträge zur Topografie," in Detlef Hofmann, ed., *Der Angriff der Gegenwart auf die Vergangenheit: Denkmale auf dem Gelände ehemaliger Konzentrationslager* [The Assault of the Present on the Past: Memorials on the Sites of Former Concentration Camps] (Rehburg-Loccum: Evangelische Akademie Loccum, 1996), 113–31.

Bäcker delivered this text as a lecture at an academic conference about concentration camp memorials hosted by the Protestant Academy in the North German town of Loccum.

The Mauthausen concentration camp system, which included several subcamps, was established in 1938 in the town of Mauthausen, near Linz, only months after Austria was annexed by Nazi Germany. Its location was chosen for the local quarries, where prisoners were forced to work under inhumane and often fatal conditions. The complex also included underground armaments factories. 190,000 people were held in Mauthausen and its subcamps, and at least 90,000 were killed there. Today, it is the most important memorial site in Austria, and its maintenance and administration have improved dramatically in the years since Bäcker gave this lecture.

In *Aktion K,* the *"Bullet Campaign,"* between 2,000 and 5,000 Russian prisoners of war and forced laborers suspected of political activities and sabotage were executed or condemned to death by being confined without food or shelter. The exact number of these prisoners is unknown because they were not registered in the camp's records.

The phrase *"euthanasia campaign"* refers to the Nazi regime's systematic killing of around 250,000 adults and children with mental and physical disabilities. In *Operation 14f13,* concentration camp prisoners were sent to so-called "euthanasia" centers to be killed.

NOTES: originally published as "Notizen," in *Wespennest* 68 (1987), 77–8.

"A Volk on a quest ..." quotes political jargon from a text that Bäcker published as a reporter during the Nazi era.

Ernst Röhm was the leader of the SA (abbreviation for *Sturmabteilung,* Storm Division, also known as Storm Troopers). He was assassinated in 1934 when other Nazi leaders, including Hitler, believed that he posed a threat to their plans for dominating Germany.

Hermann Göring was a high-ranking Nazi official, designated as Hitler's successor, who was known for his excessive consumption habits.

The *Weimar Republic* is the name given to the German government that ruled from 1919 until January 30, 1933, when Hitler was chosen to be Chancellor and quickly destroyed the Republic's democratic institutions and civil rights. It took on this name because its constitution was signed in the city of *Weimar*, which is associated with writers like Goethe and Schiller, who made it a literary and cultural center around

1800. The *Buchenwald* concentration camp was established outside of Weimar in 1937. 250,000 prisoners were held there; about 56,000 were killed.

CONCRETE POETRY: "konkrete dichtung," in Neue Galerie der Stadt Linz, ed., *Die Künstlervereinigung März, 1913–1973* (Linz: Künstlervereinigung März, 1973), 84–86.

Bob Cobbing was a leading British concrete and visual poet. *Josef Bauer* and *Fritz Lichtenauer* were Linz-based artists. The Swiss poet Eugen Gomringer and Austrian poet Friedrich Achleitner both named some of their concrete poems "constellations."

ON THE ARPEIRON: RESPONSE TO A SURVEY ABOUT THE AVANT-GARDE TODAY: "Vom Arpeiron," in Thomas Eder and Klaus Kastberger, eds., *Der lange Atem der österreichischen Avantgarde* [The Long Life of the Austrian Avant-Garde] (Vienna: Zsolnay, 2000), 148–51.

Bäcker's title is a portmanteau combining the name of Jean Arp and the Ancient Greek term for the boundless and infinite, *apeiron*.

"THE TRUTH OF KILLING": AN INTERVIEW: Judith Veichtlbauer and Stephan Steiner, "Die Wahrheit des Mordens: Ein Interview," in Thomas Eder and Klaus Kastberger, eds., *Die Rampe Porträt: Heimrad Bäcker* (Linz: Trauner, 2001), 85–8.

Conducted by the literary critics Judith Veichtlbauer and Stephan Steiner, an abridged version of the interview was originally published in the Viennese weekly magazine *Der Falter* in 1995 in conjunction with the Vienna exhibition *200 Days and One Century*, which focused on the 200 days between the liberation of Auschwitz and the United States' nuclear attack on Hiroshima.

SEASCAPE: *SEESTÜCK* (Linz: Neue Texte, 1985). English translation first published as *SEASCAPE*, trans. Patrick Greaney (New York: Ugly Duckling Presse, 2013).

TRANSCRIPT Z: "Nachschrift Z" in *Der Behinderte* 2 (1995), 37–40. Based on handwritten notes in Bäcker's papers in the Austrian National Library (ÖLA 214/03, Gruppe 1.1), two changes were made to the text: the spacing of the ninth entry and the addition of Gideon Greif to the bibliography.

IMAGE CHECKLIST

All images used in this book are by Heimrad Bäcker and appear courtesy of Michael Merighi; photos copyright © mumok, Museum moderner Kunst Stiftung Ludwig Wien.

1. Closing Ceremonies, 1943/1944 (7 × 5 inches)

2. Traces of Labor in the Wiener Graben Quarry in the Mauthausen Concentration Camp, n.d. ($15\,^7/_8$ × 12 inches)

3. Stone Crusher in the Gusen Concentration Camp (Condition after 1945), 1975 (12 × $17\,^1/_2$ inches)

4. Gatehouse to the Gusen Concentration Camp (Condition 1945-1993), 1975 (5 × 7 inches)

5. Tunnels of "Rock Crystal," Underground Factory for Production of Me 262 Jet Fighter, in St. Georgen (Concentration Camp Mauthausen/Gusen II), n.d. ($11\,^1/_4$ × $8\,^1/_4$ inches)

6. Memorial Marker Mauthausen Concentration Camp 1968, 1968 (3 × 5 inches)

7. Memorial Marker Mauthausen Concentration Camp 1995, 1995 (4 × 6 inches)

8. "Death Stairs" in the Wiener Graben Quarry of the Mauthausen Concentration Camp, 1970–1975 (5 × $3\,^1/_2$ inches)

9. Technological Remnants, n.d. (4 $^7/_{16}$ × 2 $^1/_{16}$ inches)

10. Iron Remnants in the Foundation of the Great Hall of the Mauthausen Concentration Camp, n.d. (15 $^7/_8$ × 12 inches)

11. Photographs from Television: Gestapo Cellar in Cologne, n.d. (9 $^1/_2$ × 7 inches)

ACKNOWLEDGMENTS

I would like to thank Thomas Eder, Heimrad Bäcker's literary executor, and Michael Merighi, Heimrad Bäcker's son and the executor of his artistic estate, for their support of this book; Gabrielle Kaiser, Christopher Laferl, and Sabine Zelger for discussions about Bäcker and the translations; and Claudia Freiberger and Marie Therese Hochwartner, both from the Museum of Modern Art (MUMOK) in Vienna, for their assistance with Bäcker's photographs.

I am grateful to Matvei Yankelevich and Henry Gifford for their helpful comments on the translations and to Judith Veichtlbauer and Stephan Steiner for giving their permission to translate their 1995 interview with Bäcker.

Research for the translation was funded in part by the University of Colorado Boulder's Arts and Sciences Fund for Excellence, and the publication was supported by the University of Colorado Boulder's Kayden Research Grant and by the Austrian Federal Ministry for Art, Culture, the Civil Service, and Sport.

HEIMRAD BÄCKER (1925–2003) was a poet, photographer, and the editor of the journal *neue texte* and, together with Margret Bäcker, the avant-garde publisher edition neue texte. As a teenager, he was active in the regional leadership of the Hitler Youth and joined the Nazi Party when he was eighteen. After the war, he completed his doctoral studies in philosophy with a dissertation on Karl Jaspers. The author of seven books of poetry, his work has been translated into French, Swedish, and Turkish. English translations of his work include *transcript* (Dalkey Archive) and *SEASCAPE* (Ugly Duckling Presse). Solo exhibitions of his photographic and sculptural works have taken place at The Upper Austrian State Museum (2002/2003), Museum of Contemporary Art Denver (2013/2014), the Museum of Modern Art in Vienna (2019/2020), and the Munich Documentation Center for the History of National Socialism (2021).

PATRICK GREANEY is Professor of German Studies at the University of Colorado Boulder. He is the co-editor and translator of *An Austrian Avant-Garde* (Les Figues Press) and the author of *Untimely Beggar: Poverty and Power from Baudelaire to Benjamin* and *Quotational Practices: Repeating the Future in Contemporary Art*, both from University of Minnesota Press. He is the co-translator (with Vincent Kling) of Heimrad Bäcker's *transcript* (Dalkey Archive).

ISBN 978-1-959708-07-0
LCCN: 2024937406

First Edition, 2024 — 1200 copies

Winter Editions, Brooklyn, New York
wintereditions.net

The publication of this book was supported
by grants from the University of Colorado
Boulder's Kayden Research Fund and from
the Republic of Austria's Federal Ministry of
Arts, Culture, Civil Service, and Sport.

= Federal Ministry
Republic of Austria
Arts, Culture,
Civil Service and Sport

WE is supported by subscribers and individual donors, and extends
special thanks to recent Supporting Subscribers: Anonymous,
Anonymous (in memory of the Beaubiens), Yevgeniy Fiks, and
Elizabeth T. Gray, Jr.

WE books are typeset in Heldane, a renaissance-inspired serif
designed by Kris Sowersby for Klim Type Foundry, and Zirkon,
a contemporary gothic designed by Tobias Rechsteiner for Grilli
Type. The layout and covers are done by the editor following a
series design created by Andrew Bourne. This book was printed
and bound in Lithuania by BALTO print.

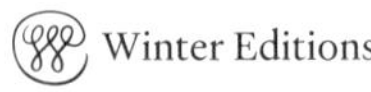 Winter Editions

Emily Simon, IN MANY WAYS

Garth Graeper, THE SKY BROKE MORE

Robert Desnos, NIGHT OF LOVELESS NIGHTS, tr. Lewis Warsh

Richard Hell, WHAT JUST HAPPENED

Marina Tëmkina & Michel Gérard, BOYS FIGHT
[co-published with Alder & Frankia]

Claire DeVoogd, VIA

Monica McClure, THE GONE THING

Ahmad Almallah, BORDER WISDOM

Hélio Oiticica, SECRET POETICS, tr. Rebecca Kosick
[co-published with Soberscove Press]

Heimrad Bäcker, DOCUMENTARY POETRY, tr. Patrick Greaney

Robert Fitterman, CREVE COEUR

Karla Kelsey, TRANSCENDENTAL FACTORY: FOR MINA LOY

Alan Gilbert, THE EVERYDAY LIFE OF DESIGN

Betsy Fagin, FIRES SEEN FROM SPACE

POSTCARDS FROM THE SIEGE, ed. Polina Barskova
[co-published with Blavatnik Archive]